GOD'S PROMISE FOR TODAY

SELECTED SCRIPTURE FOR EACH DAY OF THE YEAR PLUS 365 GEMS OF WISDOM

Benjamin R. DeJong

D0862128

BAKER BOOK HOUSE
Grand Rapids, Michigan

Preface

The Reverend De Jong is a pastor, a shepherd of God's flock, with many years of experience. It is good to know him as a personal friend and fellow Christian. This devotional book reflects his understanding of the needs of God's children and his fervent belief that Scripture alone can answer those needs. I heartily commend this book to you who desire God's light to be shed upon each day.

John Miles, *President*
Grand Rapids School
of the Bible and Music

January

JANUARY 1

The meek will He guide in judgment: and the meek will He teach His way (Ps. 25:9).

He maketh me to lie down in green pastures: He leadeth me beside the still waters (Ps. 23:2).

Thou wilt guide me with Thy counsel, and afterward receive me to glory (Ps. 73:24).

And thine ears shall hear a word behind thee, saying, This is the way, walk ye in it, when ye turn to the right hand, and when ye turn to the left (Isa. 30:21).

For Thy mercy is great above the heavens: and Thy truth reacheth unto the clouds (Ps. 108:4).

GOD'S PROMISE FOR TODAY

For this God is our God for ever and ever: He will be our guide even unto death (Ps. 48:14).

"God guides our stops as well as our steps."

JANUARY 2

Be kindly affectioned one to another with brotherly love; in honour preferring one another (Rom. 12:10).

Love suffereth long, and is kind; love envieth not; love vaunteth not itself, is not puffed up (I Cor. 13:4).

And be ye kind one to another, tender hearted, forgiving one another, even as God for Christ's sake hath forgiven you (Eph. 4:32).

Rejoice with them that do rejoice, and weep with them that weep (Rom. 12:15).

But now abideth faith, hope, love, these three; and the greatest of these is love (I Cor. 13:13, RV).

GOD'S PROMISE FOR TODAY

My little children, let us not love in word, neither in tongue; but in deed and in truth (I John 3:18).

"Salvation without good works is shameful."

JANUARY 3

For the froward is abomination to the Lord; but His secret is with the righteous (Prov. 3:32).

These six things doth the Lord hate: yea, seven are an abomination to Him: a proud look, a lying tongue, and hands that shed innocent blood, a heart that deviseth wicked imaginations, feet that be swift in running to mischief, a false witness that speaketh lies, and he that soweth discord among brethren (Prov. 6:16-19).

The sacrifice of the wicked is an abomination to the Lord: but the prayer of the upright is his delight. The way of the wicked is an abomination unto the Lord: but He loveth him that followeth after righteousness. The thoughts of the wicked are an abomination to the Lord: but the words of the pure are pleasant words (Prov. 15:8, 9, 26).

GOD'S PROMISE FOR TODAY

Lying lips are abomination to the Lord: but they that deal truly are His delight (Prov. 12:22).

"Lying and stealing live next door to each other."

JANUARY 4

Not every one that saith unto Me, Lord, Lord, shall enter into the kingdom of heaven; but he that doeth the will of My Father which is in heaven (Matt. 7:21).

For whosoever shall do the will of My Father which is in heaven, the same is my brother, and sister, and mother (Matt. 12:50).

If ye know these things, happy are ye if ye do them (John 13:17).

For not the hearers of the law are justified before God, but the doers shall be justified (Rom. 2:13).

And the world passeth away, and the lust thereof: but he that doeth the will of God abideth for ever (I John 2:17).

"Intentions, like eggs, soon spoil unless hatched."

JANUARY 5

And they that know Thy name will put their trust in Thee: for Thou, Lord, hast not forsaken them that seek Thee (Ps. 9:10).

All the paths of the Lord are mercy and truth unto such as keep His covenant and His testimonies (Ps. 25:10).

The mercy of the Lord is from everlasting to everlasting upon them that fear Him, and His righteousness unto children's children (Ps. 103:17).

Faithful is He that calleth you, who also will do it (I Thess. 5:24).

And sent his servant at supper time to say to them that were bidden, Come; for all things are now ready (Luke 14:17).

GOD'S PROMISE FOR TODAY

All the promises of God in Him are yea, and in Him Amen (II Cor. 1:20).

"We find in life exactly what we are putting into it."

JANUARY 6

The Lord is nigh unto all them that call upon Him, to all that call upon Him in truth (Ps. 145:18).

But thou, when thou prayest, enter into thy closet, and when thou hast shut the door, pray to thy Father which is in secret; and thy Father which seeth in secret shall reward thee openly (Matt. 6:6).

Jesus saith unto him, I am the way, the truth and the life: no man cometh unto the Father, but by Me (John 14:6).

Let us therefore come boldly unto the throne of grace, that we may obtain mercy, and find grace to help in time of need (Heb. 4:16).

GOD'S PROMISE FOR TODAY

Draw nigh to God and He will draw nigh to you (James 4:8).

"Pray hardest when it is hardest to pray."

JANUARY 7

Who hath despised the day of small things? (Zech. 4:10).

And it came to pass at the seventh time, that he said, behold, there ariseth a little cloud out of the sea like a man's hand . . . and there was a great rain (I Kings 18:44a, 45b).

And the Syrians had brought away captive out of the land of Israel a little maid . . . and she said unto her mistress, Would God my lord were with the prophet that is in Samaria! for he would recover him of his leprosy . . . then went he down . . . and he was clean (II Kings 5:2, 3, 14).

Take us the foxes, the little foxes, that spoil the vines: for our vines have tender grapes (Song of Sol. 2:15).

GOD'S PROMISE FOR TODAY

For yet a little while, and He that shall come will come, and will not tarry (Heb. 10:37).

"Little is much, if God is in it."

JANUARY 8

I am a companion of all them that fear Thee, and of them that keep Thy precepts (Ps. 119:63).

Behold, how good and how pleasant it is for brethren to dwell together in unity! . . . for there the Lord commanded the blessing, even life for evermore (Ps. 133:1, 3b).

Can two walk together, except they be agreed? (Amos 3:3).

Let us consider one another to provoke unto love and to good works (Heb. 10:24).

GOD'S PROMISE FOR TODAY

So shall we ever be with the Lord. Wherefore comfort one another with these words (I Thess. 4:17b, 18).

"The best way to wipe out a friendship is to sponge on it."

JANUARY 9

Trust in the Lord and do good; so shalt thou dwell in the land, and verily thou shalt be fed (Ps. 37:3).

Delight thyself also in the Lord; and He shall give thee the desires of thine heart (Ps. 37:4).

Commit thy way unto the Lord; trust also in Him; and He shall bring it to pass (Ps. 37:5).

Rest in the Lord, and wait patiently for Him (Ps. 37:7a).

The Lord knoweth the days of the upright: and their inheritance shall be forever (Ps. 37:18).

GOD'S PROMISE FOR TODAY

The steps of a good man are ordered by the Lord: and he delighteth in His way (Ps. 37:23).

"Men are known by the way they walk, talk, and balk."

JANUARY 10

The Lord taketh pleasure in them that fear Him (Ps. 147:11).

The fear of the Lord is the beginning of knowledge: but fools despise wisdom and instruction (Prov. 1:7).

Fear the Lord and depart from evil (Prov. 3:7).

Better is a little with the fear of the Lord than great treasure and trouble therewith (Prov. 15:16).

A woman that feareth the Lord, she shall be praised (Prov. 31:30).

GOD'S PROMISE FOR TODAY

Work out your own salvation with fear and trembling. For it is God which worketh in you both to will and to do of His good pleasure (Phil. 2:12b, 13).

"The men that trust God are the men that can be trusted."

JANUARY 11

The Lord is longsuffering, and of great mercy, forgiving iniquity and transgression (Num. 14:18).

The Lord will command His lovingkindness in the daytime, and in the night His song shall be with me (Ps. 42:8).

God commendeth His love toward us, in that, while we were yet sinners, Christ died for us (Rom. 5:8).

God, who is rich in mercy, for His great love wherewith He loved us, even when we were dead in sins, hath quickened us together with Christ (Eph. 2:4, 5).

If we believe not, yet He abideth faithful: He cannot deny Himself (II Tim. 2:13).

GOD'S PROMISE FOR TODAY

The God of love and peace shall be with you (II Cor. 13:11).

"You may depend upon the Lord; may He depend upon you?"

JANUARY 12

In Him we live, and move, and have our being (Acts 17:28).

We know that all things work together for good to them that love God (Rom. 8:28).

The Lord is faithful, who shall establish you, and keep you from evil (II Thess. 3:3).

The eyes of the Lord are over the righteous, and His ears are open to their prayers: who is he that will harm you, if ye be followers of that which is good? (I Peter 3:12, 13).

And he answered, Fear not: for they that be with us are more than they that be with them (II Kings 6:16).

GOD'S PROMISE FOR TODAY

The Lord knoweth how to deliver the godly out of temptation (II Peter 2:9).

"Daily prayers lessen daily cares."

JANUARY 13

They shall be abundantly satisfied with the fatness of Thy house: and Thou shalt make them drink of the river of Thy pleasures (Ps. 36:8).

I am come that they might have life, and that they might have it more abundantly (John 10:10).

And God is able to make all grace abound toward you: that ye, always having all sufficiency in all things, may abound to every good work (II Cor. 9:8).

Now unto Him that is able to do exceedingly abundantly above all that we ask or think, according to the power that worketh in us (Eph. 3:20).

For so an entrance shall be ministered unto you abundantly into the everlasting kingdom of our Lord and Saviour Jesus Christ (II Peter 1:11).

GOD'S PROMISE FOR TODAY

But my God shall supply all your need according to His riches in glory by Christ Jesus (Phil. 4:19).

"Jesus lived that He might die, and died that we might live."

JANUARY 14

Who shall ascend into the hill of the Lord? or who shall stand in His holy place? (Ps. 24:3).

He that hath clean hands, and a pure heart: who hath not lifted up his soul unto vanity, nor sworn deceitfully (Ps. 24:4).

Open ye the gates, that the righteous nation which keepeth the truth may enter in (Isa. 26:2).

I am the door: by Me if any man enter in, he shall be saved, and shall go in and out, and find pasture (John 10:9).

By whom also we have access by faith into this grace wherein we stand, and rejoice in hope of the glory of God (Rom. 5:2).

For through Him we both have access by one Spirit unto the Father (Eph. 2:18).

GOD'S PROMISE FOR TODAY

In Whom we have boldness and access with confidence by the faith of him (Eph. 3:12).

"Satan trembles when he sees the weakest saint on his knees."

JANUARY 15

For I say unto you, That except your righteousness shall exceed the righteousness of the scribes and Pharisees, ye shall in no case enter into the kingdom of heaven (Matt. 5:20).

Verily I say unto you, Whosoever shall not receive the kingdom of God as a little child, he shall not enter therein (Mark 10:15).

Now this I say, brethren, that flesh and blood cannot inherit the kingdom of God; neither doth corruption inherit incorruption (I Cor. 15:50).

And there shall in no wise enter into it any thing that defileth, neither whatsoever worketh abomination, or maketh a lie: but they which are written in the Lamb's book of life (Rev. 21:27).

GOD'S PROMISE FOR TODAY

Know ye not that the unrighteous shall not inherit the kingdom of God? (I Cor. 6:9).

"The best way to prove godliness is by God-like-ness."

JANUARY 16

And the Angel of God, which went before the camp of Israel, removed and went behind them; and the pillar of the cloud went from before their face, and stood behind them (Exod. 14:19).

For He shall give His angels charge over thee, to keep thee in all thy ways (Ps. 91:11).

My God hath sent His angel, and hath shut the lions' mouths, that they have not hurt me: forasmuch as before Him innocency was found in me; and also before thee, O king, have I done no hurt (Dan. 6:22).

And, behold, the angel of the Lord came upon him, and a light shined in the prison: and he smote Peter on the side, and raised him up, saying, Arise up quickly. And his chains fell off from his hands (Acts 12:7).

For there stood by me this night the angel of God, Whose I am and Whom I serve (Acts 27:23).

GOD'S PROMISE FOR TODAY

Are they not all ministering spirits, sent forth to minister for them who shall be heirs of salvation? (Heb. 1:14).

" 'They say' is a tough old liar."

JANUARY 17

And when they bring you before the synagogues, and the rulers, and the authorities, be not anxious how or what ye shall answer, or what ye shall say: for the Holy Spirit shall teach you in that very hour what ye ought to say (Luke 12:11, 12).

And which of you by being anxious can add a cubit unto the measure of his life? If then ye are not able to do even that which is least, why are ye anxious concerning the rest? (Luke 12:25, 26).

But I would have you to be free from cares (I Cor. 7:32).

In nothing be anxious; but in everything by prayer and supplication with thanksgiving let your requests be made known unto God (Phil. 4:6).

GOD'S PROMISE FOR TODAY

Casting all your anxiety upon Him, because He careth for you (I Peter 5:7).

"When faith goes to market it always takes a basket."

JANUARY 18

Thou shalt not follow a multitude to do evil; neither shalt thou speak in a cause to decline after many to wrest judgment (Exod. 23:2).

Take heed to thyself, lest thou make a covenant with the inhabitants of the land whither thou goest, lest it be for a snare in the midst of thee (Exod. 34:12).

Enter not into the path of the wicked, and go not in the way of evil men (Prov. 4:14).

Be not thou envious against evil men, neither desire to be with them (Prov. 24:1).

Be ye not unequally yoked together with unbelievers: for what fellowship hath righteousness with unrighteousness? and what communion hath light with darkness? (II Cor. 6:14).

GOD'S PROMISE FOR TODAY

Blessed is the man that walketh not in the counsel of the ungodly, nor standeth in the way of sinners, nor sitteth in the seat of the scornful (Ps. 1:1).

"Friendships cemented together with sin do not hold."

JANUARY 19

Depart ye, depart ye, go ye out from thence, touch no unclean thing; go ye out of the midst of her; be ye clean, that bear the vessels of the Lord (Isa. 52:11).

If ye were of the world, the world would love his own; but because ye are not of the world, but I have chosen you out of the world, therefore the world hateth you (John 15:19).

And with many other words did he testify and exhort, saying, Save yourselves from this untoward generation (Acts 2:40).

Now we command you, brethren, in the name of our Lord Jesus Christ, that ye withdraw yourselves from every brother that walketh disorderly, and not after the tradition which he received of us (II Thess. 3:6).

GOD'S PROMISE FOR TODAY

And have no fellowship with the unfruitful works of darkness, but rather reprove them (Eph. 5:11).

"The world doesn't need a definition of religion as badly as it needs a demonstration."

JANUARY 20

Then will I teach transgressors Thy ways; and sinners shall be converted unto Thee (Ps. 51:13).

Turn us again, O God of hosts, and cause Thy face to shine; and we shall be saved (Ps. 80:7).

Wilt Thou not revive us again: that Thy people may rejoice in Thee? (Ps. 85:6).

Until the Spirit be poured upon us from on high, and the wilderness be a fruitful field, and the fruitful field be counted for a forest (Isa. 32:15).

O Lord, I have heard Thy speech, and was afraid: O Lord, revive Thy work in the midst of the years, in the midst of the years make known; in wrath remember mercy (Hab. 3:2).

GOD'S PROMISE FOR TODAY

Restore unto me the joy of Thy salvation; and uphold me with Thy free Spirit (Ps. 51:12).

"Tell me your company and I'll tell you what you are."

JANUARY 21

For the eyes of the Lord run to and fro throughout the whole earth, to shew Himself strong in the behalf of them whose heart is perfect toward Him (II Chron. 16:9).

He shall cover thee with His feathers, and under His wings shalt thou trust: His truth shall be thy shield and buckler (Ps. 91:4).

As the mountains are round about Jerusalem, so the Lord is round about His people from henceforth even for ever (Ps. 125:2).

For I, saith the Lord, will be unto her a wall of fire round about, and will be the glory in the midst of her. (Zech. 2:5).

But there shall not a hair of your head perish (Luke 21:18).

GOD'S PROMISE FOR TODAY

The angel of the Lord encampeth round about them that fear Him, and delivereth them (Ps. 34:7).

"The most thankful people are the humblest."

JANUARY 22

Forever, O Lord, Thy word is settled in heaven (Ps. 119:89).

The grass withereth, the flower fadeth: but the word of our God shall stand for ever (Isa. 40:8).

For verily I say unto you, till heaven and earth pass, one jot or one tittle shall in no wise pass from the law, till all be fulfilled (Matt. 5:18).

But the word of the Lord endureth for ever. And this is the word which by the gospel is preached unto you (I Peter 1:25).

For He satisfieth the longing soul, and filleth the hungry soul with goodness (Ps. 107:9).

GOD'S PROMISE FOR TODAY

Heaven and earth shall pass away, but My words shall not pass away (Matt. 24:35).

"Where the devil cannot go himself he sends a gossiper."

The statutes of the Lord are right, rejoicing the heart: the commandment of the Lord is pure, enlightening the eyes (Ps. 19:8).

The entrance of Thy words giveth light; it giveth understanding unto the simple (Ps. 119:130).

For the commandment is a lamp; and the law is light; and reproofs of instruction are the way of life (Prov. 6:23).

We have also a more sure word of prophecy; whereunto ye do well that ye take heed, as unto a light that shineth in a dark place, until the day dawn, and the daystar arise in your hearts (II Peter 1:19).

GOD'S PROMISE FOR TODAY

Thy word is a lamp unto my feet, and a light unto my path (Ps. 119:105).

"The only objection against the Bible is a bad life."

JANUARY 24

Now ye are clean through the word which I have spoken unto you (John 15:3).

Sanctify them through Thy truth: Thy word is truth (John 17:17).

That He might sanctify and cleanse it with the washing of water by the word (Eph. 5:26).

Seeing ye have purified your souls in obeying the truth through the Spirit unto unfeigned love of the brethren, see that ye love one another with a pure heart fervently (I Peter 1:22).

For we are members of His body, of His flesh, and of His bones (Eph. 5:30).

Therefore to him that knoweth to do good, and doeth it not, to him it is sin (James 4:17).

GOD'S PROMISE FOR TODAY

Wherewithal shall a young man cleanse his way? by taking heed thereto according to Thy word (Ps. 119:9).

"There are two parts to the gospel: believing it,
and behaving it."

JANUARY 25

But these are written, that ye might believe that Jesus is the

Christ, the Son of God: and that believing ye might have life through His name (John 20:31).

For whatsoever things were written aforetime were written for our learning, that we through patience and comfort of the Scriptures might have hope (Rom. 15:4).

Now all these things happened unto them for ensamples; and they are written for our admonition, upon whom the ends of the world are come (I Cor. 10:11).

These things have I written unto you that believe on the name of the Son of God; that ye may know that ye have eternal life, and that ye may believe on the name of the Son of God (I John 5:13).

GOD'S PROMISE FOR TODAY

Thy word have I hid in my heart, that I might not sin against Thee (Ps. 119:11).

"The Christian is free, but not free to sin."

JANUARY 26

And it shall be with him, and he shall read therein all the days of his life; that he may learn to fear the Lord his God, to keep all the words of this law and these statutes, to do them (Deut. 17:19).

Seek ye out of the book of the Lord, and read: no one of these shall fail, none shall want her mate: for my mouth it hath commanded, and His Spirit it hath gathered them (Isa. 34:16).

These were more noble than those in Thessalonica, in that they received the word with all readiness of mind, and searched the Scriptures daily, whether those things were so (Acts 17:11).

For whatsoever things were written aforetime were written for our learning, that we through patience and comfort of the Scriptures might have hope (Rom. 15:4).

GOD'S PROMISE FOR TODAY

Search the Scriptures; for in them ye think ye have eternal life: and they are they which testify of Me (John 5:39).

"There are multitudes whose Bibles are 'read' only on the edges."

JANUARY 27

And ye shall serve the Lord your God, and He shall bless thy bread and thy water; and I will take sickness away from the midst of thee (Exod. 23:25).

He should have fed them also with the finest of wheat: and with honey out of the rock should I have satisfied thee (Ps. 81:16).

Then shall He give the rain of thy seed, that thou shalt sow the ground withal; and bread of the increase of the earth, and it shall be fat and plenteous: in that day shall thy cattle feed in large pastures (Isa. 30:23).

Behold, the days come, saith the Lord, that the ploughman shall overtake the reaper, and the treader of grapes him that soweth seed; and the mountains shall drop sweet wine, and all the hills shall melt (Amos 9:13).

GOD'S PROMISE FOR TODAY

But seek ye first the kingdom of God and His righteousness; and all these things shall be added unto you (Matt. 6:33).

"The millionaires in eternity are the givers in time."

JANUARY 28

Therefore, seeing we have this ministry, as we have received mercy, we faint not (II Cor. 4:1).

For which cause we faint not; but though our outward man perish, yet the inward man is renewed day by day (II Cor. 4:16).

Wherefore I desire that ye faint not at my tribulations for you, which is your glory (Eph. 3:13).

And ye have forgotten the exhortation which speaketh unto you as unto children, My son, despise not thou the chastening of the Lord, nor faint when thou art rebuked of Him (Heb. 12:5).

And hast borne, and hast patience, and for My name's sake hast laboured, and hast not fainted (Rev. 2:3).

GOD'S PROMISE FOR TODAY

My son, despise not the chastening of the Lord; neither be weary of His correction (Prov. 3:11).

"Sanctified afflictions are spiritual promotions."

JANUARY 29

And Elisha prayed, and said, Lord, I pray Thee, open his eyes, that he may see. And the Lord opened the eyes of the young man; and he saw: and, behold, the mountain was full of horses and chariots of fire round about Elisha (II Kings 6:17).

I have heard of Thee by the hearing of the ear; but now mine eye seeth Thee (Job 42:5).

Yet a little while, and the world seeth Me no more; but ye see Me: because I live, ye shall live also (John 14:19).

All things that the Father hath are Mine; therefore said I, that He shall take of Mine, and shall shew it unto you (John 16:15).

By faith he forsook Egypt, not fearing the wrath of the king: for he endured, as seeing Him Who is invisible (Heb. 11:27).

GOD'S PROMISE FOR TODAY

Blessed are the pure in heart: for they shall see God (Matt. 5:8).

"Christians never meet for the last time."

JANUARY 30

They looked unto Him, and were lightened: and their faces were not ashamed (Ps. 34:5).

Then they took away the stone from the place where the dead was laid. And Jesus lifted up His eyes, and said, Father, I thank Thee that Thou hast heard Me (John 11:41).

These words spake Jesus, and lifted up His eyes to heaven, and said, Father, the hour is come; glorify Thy Son, that Thy Son also may glorify Thee (John 17:1).

And while they looked steadfastly toward heaven as He went up, behold, two men stood by them in white apparel (Acts 1:10).

But he, being full of the Holy Ghost, looked up steadfastly into heaven, and saw the glory of God, and Jesus standing on the right hand of God (Acts 7:55).

GOD'S PROMISE FOR TODAY

I will lift up mine eyes unto the hills, from whence cometh my help. My help cometh from the Lord, which made heaven and earth (Ps. 121:1, 2).

"When the outlook is bad, try the uplook."

JANUARY 31

In Whom we have boldness and access with confidence by the faith of Him (Eph. 3:12).

For they that have used the office of a deacon well purchase to themselves a good degree, and great boldness in the faith which is in Christ Jesus (I Tim. 3:13).

Let us therefore come boldly unto the throne of grace, that

we may obtain mercy, and find grace to help in time of need (Heb. 4:16).

Herein is our love made perfect, that we may have boldness in the day of judgment: because as He is, so are we in this world (I John 4:17).

GOD'S PROMISE FOR TODAY

Having therefore, brethren, boldness to enter into the holiest by the blood of Jesus (Heb. 10:19).

"If we let God guide, He will provide."

February

FEBRUARY 1

He becometh poor that dealeth with a slack hand: but the hand of the diligent maketh rich (Prov. 10:4).

The soul of the sluggard desireth, and hath nothing: but the soul of the diligent shall be made fat (Prov. 13:4).

Seest thou a man diligent in his business? he shall stand before kings; he shall not stand before mean men (Prov. 22:29).

Wherefore, beloved, seeing that ye look for such things, be diligent that ye may be found of him in peace, without spot, and blameless (II Peter 3:14).

GOD'S PROMISE FOR TODAY

That ye be not slothful, but followers of them who through faith and patience inherit the promises (Heb. 6:12).

"If the devil catches a man idle, he will set him to work."

FEBRUARY 2

Ye shall do no unrighteousness in judgment, in meteyard, in weight, or in measure (Lev. 19:35).

Just balances, just weights, a just ephah, and a just hin, shall ye have: I am the Lord your God, which brought you out of the land of Egypt (Lev. 19:36).

But thou shalt have a perfect and just weight, a perfect and just measure shalt thou have: that thy days may be lengthened in the land which the Lord thy God giveth thee (Deut. 25:15).

A false balance is abomination to the Lord: but a just weight is his delight (Prov. 11:1).

Owe no man any thing, but to love one another: for he that loveth another hath fulfilled the law (Rom. 13:8).

GOD'S PROMISE FOR TODAY

Recompense to no man evil for evil. Provide things honest in the sight of all men (Rom. 12:17).

"Sin has many tools, but a lie is a handle that fits them all."

FEBRUARY 3

Go to the ant, thou sluggard; consider her ways, and be wise (Prov. 6:6).

He that gathereth in summer is a wise son: but he that sleepeth in harvest is a son that causeth shame (Prov. 10:5).

He that tilleth his land shall be satisfied with bread: but he that followeth vain persons is void of understanding (Prov. 12:11).

Wealth gotten by vanity shall be diminished: but he that gathereth by labour shall increase (Prov. 13:11).

Love not sleep, lest thou come to poverty; open thine eyes, and thou shalt be satisfied with bread (Prov. 20:13).

GOD'S PROMISE FOR TODAY

Not slothful in business; fervent in spirit; serving the Lord (Rom. 12:11).

"Poverty is usually the side-partner of laziness."

FEBRUARY 4

The getting of treasures by a lying tongue is a vanity tossed to and fro of them that seek death (Prov. 21:6).

He that oppresseth the poor to increase his riches, and he that giveth to the rich, shall surely come to want (Prov. 22:16).

As the partridge sitteth on eggs, and hatcheth them not; so he that getteth riches, and not by right, shall leave them in the midst of his days, and at his end shall be a fool (Jer. 17:11).

Woe unto him that buildeth his house by unrighteousness, and his chambers by wrong: that useth his neighbor's service without wages, and giveth him not for his work (Jer. 22:13).

Behold, therefore I have smitten mine hand at thy dishonest gain which thou hast made, and at thy blood which hath been in the midst of thee (Ezek. 22:13).

GOD'S PROMISE FOR TODAY

Better is a little with righteousness, than great revenues without right (Prov. 16:8).

"Good works are found only in the one in whom God works."

FEBRUARY 5

He also that is slothful in his work is brother to him that is a great waster (Prov. 18:9).

I went by the field of the slothful, and by the vineyard of the man void of understanding (Prov. 24:30).

And, lo, it was all grown over with thorns, and nettles had covered the face thereof, and the stone wall thereof was broken down (Prov. 24:31).

By much slothfulness the building decayeth; and through idleness of the hands the house droppeth through (Eccles. 10:18).

For we hear that there are some which walk among you disorderly, working not at all, but are busybodies (II Thess. 3:11).

That ye be not slothful, but followers of them who through faith and patience inherit the promises (Heb. 6:12).

GOD'S PROMISE FOR TODAY

Slothfulness casteth into a deep sleep; and an idle soul shall suffer hunger (Prov. 19:15).

"A revolving fan gathers no flies."

FEBRUARY 6

Servants, be obedient to them that are your masters according to the flesh, with fear and trembling, in singleness of your heart, as unto Christ (Eph. 6:5).

Let as many servants as are under the yoke count their own masters worthy of all honour, that the name of God and His doctrine be not blasphemed (I Tim. 6:1).

Exhort servants to be obedient unto their own masters, and to please them well in all things; not answering again (Titus 2:9).

Servants, be subject to your masters with all fear; not only to the good and gentle, but also to the froward (I Peter 2:18).

GOD'S PROMISE FOR TODAY

Servants, obey in all things your masters according to the flesh; not with eyeservice, as menpleasers; but in singleness of heart, fearing God (Col. 3:22).

"Service is love in working clothes."

FEBRUARY 7

And the Lord God took the man, and put him into the garden of Eden, to dress it and to keep it (Gen. 2:15).

In the sweat of thy face shalt thou eat bread, till thou return unto the ground; for out of it wast thou taken: for dust thou art, and unto dust shalt thou return (Gen. 3:19).

Let him that stole steal no more: but rather let him labour, working with his hands the thing which is good, that he may have to give to him that needeth (Eph. 4:28).

Now them that are such we command and exhort by our Lord Jesus Christ, that with quietness they work, and eat their own bread (II Thess. 3:12).

GOD'S PROMISE FOR TODAY

Whatsoever thy hand findeth to do, do it with thy might; for there is no work, nor device, nor knowledge, nor wisdom, in the grave, whither thou goest (Eccles. 9:10).

"If you are a Christian, remember that men judge your Lord by you."

FEBRUARY 8

What profit hath a man of all his labour which he taketh under the sun? (Eccles. 1:3).

There is one alone, and there is not a second; yea, he hath neither child nor brother: yet is there no end of all his labour; neither is his eye satisfied with riches; neither saith he, for whom do I labour, and bereave my soul of good? This is also vanity, yea, it is a sore travail (Eccles. 4:8).

Wherefore do ye spend money for that which is not bread? and your labour for that which satisfieth not? (Isa. 55:2).

Labour not for the meat which perisheth, but for that meat which endureth unto everlasting life, which the Son of man shall give unto you: for Him hath God the Father sealed (John 6:27).

GOD'S PROMISE FOR TODAY

For what shall it profit a man, if he shall gain the whole world, and lose his own soul? (Mark 8:36).

"As you live so will you die, as the tree falls so will it lie."

FEBRUARY 9

He that covereth a transgression seeketh love; but he that repeateth a matter separateth very friends (Prov. 17:9).

And why beholdest thou the mote that is in thy brother's eye, but considerest not the beam that is in thine own eye? (Matt. 7:3).

Brethren, if a man be overtaken in a fault, ye which are spiritual, restore such a one in the spirit of meekness; considering thyself, lest thou also be tempted (Gal. 6:1).

And above all things have fervent charity among yourselves: for charity shall cover the multitude of sins (I Peter 4:8).

GOD'S PROMISE FOR TODAY

We then that are strong ought to bear the infirmities of the weak, and not to please ourselves (Rom. 15:1).

"If slighted, slight the slight, and love the slighter."

FEBRUARY 10

Who are thou that judgest another man's servant? to his own master he standeth or falleth; yea, he shall be holden up: for God is able to make him stand (Rom. 14:4).

Let us not therefore judge one another any more: but judge this rather, that no man put a stumblingblock or an occasion to fall in his brother's way (Rom. 14:13).

Therefore judge nothing before the time, until the Lord come, Who both will bring to light the hidden things of darkness, and will make manifest the counsels of the hearts: and then shall every man have praise of God (I Cor. 4:5).

There is one lawgiver, Who is able to save and to destroy: who art thou that judgest another? (James 4:12).

GOD'S PROMISE FOR TODAY

Judge not, that ye be not judged (Matt. 7:1).

"A ready accuser is usually a self-excuser."

FEBRUARY 11

A merry heart maketh a cheerful countenance: but by sorrow of the heart the spirit is broken (Prov. 15:13).

These things I have spoken unto you, that in Me ye might have peace. In the world ye shall have tribulation: but be of good cheer; I have overcome the world (John 16:33).

Wherefore, sirs, be of good cheer: for I believe God, that it shall be even as it was told me (Acts 27:25).

Then were they all of good cheer, and they also took some meat (Acts 27:36).

And the night following the Lord stood by him, and said, Be of good cheer, Paul: for as thou hast testified of Me in Jerusalem, so must thou bear witness also at Rome (Acts 23:11).

GOD'S PROMISE FOR TODAY

A merry heart doeth good like a medicine: but a broken spirit drieth the bones. (Prov. 17:22).

"Of all the things you wear, your expression is the most important."

FEBRUARY 12

And if it seem evil unto you to serve the Lord, choose you this day whom ye will serve; whether the gods which your fathers served that were on the other side of the flood, or the gods of the Amorites, in whose land ye dwell: but as for me and my house, we will serve the Lord (Josh. 24:15).

And Ruth said, Intreat me not to leave thee, or to return from following after thee: for whither thou goest, I will go; and where thou lodgest, I will lodge: thy people shall be my people, and thy God my God (Ruth 1:16).

Give therefore thy servant an understanding heart to judge Thy people, that I may discern between good and bad: for who is able to judge this Thy so great a people? (I Kings 3:9).

GOD'S PROMISE FOR TODAY

Choosing rather to suffer affliction with the people of God, than to enjoy the pleasures of sin for a season (Heb. 11:25).

"The pleasures of sin are for a season; but its wages are for eternity."

FEBRUARY 13

For this is My blood of the new testament, which is shed for many for the remission of sins (Matt. 26:28).

Much more then, being now justified by His blood, we shall be saved from wrath through Him (Rom. 5:9).

How much more shall the blood of Christ, Who through the eternal Spirit offered Himself without spot to God, purge your conscience from dead works to serve the living God? (Heb. 9:14).

Forasmuch as ye know that ye were not redeemed with corruptible things, as silver and gold, from your vain conversation received by tradition from your fathers (I Peter 1:18).

But with the precious blood of Christ, as of a lamb without blemish and without spot (I Peter 1:19).

GOD'S PROMISE FOR TODAY

But if we walk in the light, as He is in the light, we have fellowship one with another, and the blood of Jesus Christ His Son cleanseth us from all sin (I John 1:7).

"A man may be almost saved yet entirely lost."

FEBRUARY 14

Then they that gladly received his word were baptized: and the same day there were added unto them about three thousand souls (Acts 2:41).

Howbeit many of them which heard the word believed; and the number of the men was about five thousand (Acts 4:4).

And believers were the more added to the Lord, multitudes both of men and women (Acts 5:14).

And the word of God increased; and the number of the disciples multiplied in Jerusalem greatly; and a great company of the priests were obedient to the faith (Acts 6:7).

And the hand of the Lord was with them: and a great number believed, and turned unto the Lord (Acts 11:21).

GOD'S PROMISE FOR TODAY

Praising God, and having favour with all the people. And the Lord added to the church daily such as should be saved (Acts 2:47).

"A religion that costs nothing does nothing."

FEBRUARY 15

And hath put all things under His feet, and gave Him to be the head over all things to the church (Eph. 1:22).

But speaking the truth in love, may grow up into Him in all things, which is the head, even Christ (Eph. 4:15).

For the husband is the head of the wife, even as Christ is the head of the church: and He is the Saviour of the body (Eph. 5:23).

And not holding the Head, from which all the body by joints and bands having nourishment ministered, and knit together, increaseth with the increase of God (Col. 2:19).

GOD'S PROMISE FOR TODAY

And He is the head of the body, the church: Who is the beginning, the first-born from the dead; that in all things He might have the preeminence (Col. 1:18).

"It is better not to be born than not to be born again."

FEBRUARY 16

Wherefore, my brethren, ye also are become dead to the law by the body of Christ; that ye should be married to another, even to Him who is raised from the dead, that we should bring forth fruit unto God (Rom. 7:4).

Know ye not that your bodies are the members of Christ? shall I then take the members of Christ, and make them the members of a harlot? God forbid (I Cor. 6:15).

Let that therefore abide in you, which ye have heard from the beginning. If that which ye have heard from the beginning shall remain in you, ye shall continue in the Son, and in the Father (I John 2:24).

GOD'S PROMISE FOR TODAY

For I am jealous over you with godly jealousy: for I have espoused you to one husband, that I may present you as a chaste virgin to Christ (II Cor. 11:2).

"Sin forsaken is the surest sign of sin forgiven."

FEBRUARY 17

Blessed are the peacemakers: for they shall be called the children of God (Matt. 5:9).

Neither can they die any more: for they are equal unto the angels; and are the children of God, being the children of the resurrection (Luke 20:36).

Because the creature itself also shall be delivered from the bondage of corruption into the glorious liberty of the children of God (Rom. 8:21).

And it shall come to pass, that in the place where it was said unto them, ye are not my people; there shall they be called the children of the living God (Rom. 9:26).

In this the children of God are manifest, and the children of the devil: whosoever doeth not righteousness is not of God, neither he that loveth not his brother (I John 3:10).

GOD'S PROMISE FOR TODAY

The Spirit itself beareth witness with our spirit, that we are the children of God (Rom. 8:16).

"The blood makes us safe. The Word makes us sure."

And if children, then heirs; heirs of God, and joint-heirs with Christ: if so be that we suffer with Him, that we may be also glorified together (Rom. 8:17).

And if ye be Christ's, then are ye Abraham's seed, and heirs according to the promise (Gal. 3:29).

Are they not all ministering spirits, sent forth to minister for them who shall be heirs of salvation? (Heb. 1:14).

Wherein God, willing more abundantly to shew unto the heirs of promise the immutability of His counsel, confirmed it by an oath (Heb. 6:17).

GOD'S PROMISE FOR TODAY

That being justified by His grace, we should be made heirs according to the hope of eternal life (Titus 3:7).

"A contented mind is a continual feast."

FEBRUARY 19

But as many as received Him, to them gave He power to become the sons of God, even to them that believe on His name (John 1:12).

Wherefore thou art no more a servant, but a son; and if a son, then an heir of God through Christ (Gal. 4:7).

That ye may be blameless and harmless, the sons of God, without rebuke, in the midst of a crooked and perverse nation, among whom ye shine as lights in the world (Phil. 2:15).

Behold, what manner of love the Father hath bestowed upon us, that we should be called the sons of God: therefore the world knoweth us not, because it knew Him not (I John 3:1).

GOD'S PROMISE FOR TODAY

For as many as are led by the Spirit of God, they are the sons of God (Romans 8:14).

"Some self-made men show poor architectural skill."

FEBRUARY 20

But Jesus turned Him about, and when He saw her, He said, Daughter, be of good comfort; thy faith hath made thee whole. And the woman was made whole from that hour (Matt. 9:22).

And when the Lord saw her, He had compassion on her, and said unto her, Weep not (Luke 7:13).

Let not your heart be troubled: ye believe in God, believe also in Me (John 14:1).

I will not leave you comfortless: I will come to you (John 14:18).

These things I have spoken unto you, that in Me ye might have peace. In the world ye shall have tribulation: but be of good cheer; I have overcome the world (John 16:33).

GOD'S PROMISE FOR TODAY

Blessed be God, even the Father of our Lord Jesus Christ, the Father of mercies, and the God of all comfort (II Cor. 1:3).

"Peace rules the day when Christ rules the mind."

FEBRUARY 21

And they heard the voice of the Lord God walking in the garden in the cool of the day: and Adam and his wife hid themselves from the presence of the Lord God amongst the trees of the garden (Gen. 3:8).

When I saw among the spoils a goodly Babylonish garment, and two hundred shekels of silver, and a wedge of gold of fifty shekels weight, then I coveted them, and took them; and, behold, they are hid in the earth in the midst of my tent, and the silver under it (Josh. 7:21).

Woe unto them that seek deep to hide their counsel from the Lord, and their works are in the dark, and they say, who seeth us? and who knoweth us? (Isa. 29:15).

GOD'S PROMISE FOR TODAY

He that covereth his sins shall not prosper: but whoso confesseth and forsaketh them shall have mercy (Prov. 28:13).

"Backsliding is a paralysis of the knees."

FEBRUARY 22

And the children of Israel did secretly those things that were not right against the Lord their God, and they built them high places in all their cities, from the tower of the watchmen to the fenced city (II Kings 17:9).

In the dark they dig through houses, which they had marked for themselves in the daytime: they knew not the light (Job 24:16).

Thou hast set our iniquities before Thee, our secret sins in the light of Thy countenance (Ps. 90:8).

Then said He unto me, Son of man, hast thou seen what the ancients of the house of Israel do in the dark, every man in the chambers of his imagery? for they say, the Lord seeth us not; the Lord hath forsaken the earth (Ezek. 8:12).

GOD'S PROMISE FOR TODAY

Who can understand his errors? cleanse Thou me from secret faults (Ps. 19:12).

"A loose tongue often gets his owner in a tight place."

FEBRUARY 23

Whosoever therefore shall confess Me before men, him will I confess also before My Father which is in heaven (Matt. 10:32).

Also I say unto you, Whosoever shall confess me before men, him shall the Son of man also confess before the angels of God (Luke 12:8).

That if thou shalt confess with thy mouth the Lord Jesus and shall believe in thine heart that God hath raised Him from the dead, thou shalt be saved (Rom. 10:9).

And that every tongue should confess that Jesus Christ is Lord, to the glory of God the Father (Phil. 2:11).

Whosoever denieth the Son, the same hath not the Father: he that confesseth the Son hath the Father also (I John 2:23).

GOD'S PROMISE FOR TODAY

Whosoever shall confess that Jesus is the Son of God, God dwelleth in him and he in God (I John 4:15).

"Carve your name on hearts, not on marble."

FEBRUARY 24

For our rejoicing is this, the testimony of our conscience, that in simplicity and godly sincerity, not with fleshly wisdom, but by the grace of God, we have had our conversation in the world, and more abundantly to you-ward (II Cor. 1:12).

Now the end of the commandment is charity out of a pure heart, and of a good conscience, and of faith unfeigned (I Tim. 1:5).

Holding faith, and a good conscience, which some having put away, concerning faith have made shipwreck (I Tim. 1:19).

Having a good conscience; that, whereas they speak evil of you, as of evil doers, they may be ashamed that falsely accuse your good conversation in Christ (I Peter 3:16).

And herein do I exercise myself, to have always a conscience void of offence toward God, and toward men (Acts 24:16).

"Trust that man in nothing who has not conscience in everything."

FEBRUARY 25

Better is little with the fear of the Lord, than great treasure and trouble therewith (Prov. 15:16).

And the soldiers likewise demanded of him, saying, and what shall we do? And he said unto them, do violence to no man, neither accuse any falsely; and be content with your wages (Luke 3:14).

Not that I speak in respect of want: for I have learned in whatsoever state I am, therewith to be content (Phil. 4:11).

And having food and raiment, let us be therewith content (I Tim. 6:8).

Let your conversation be without covetousness; and be content with such things as ye have: for He hath said, I will never leave thee, nor forsake thee (Heb. 13:5).

GOD'S PROMISE FOR TODAY

But godliness with contentment is great gain (I Tim. 6:6).

"He who tolerates the devil soon endorses the devil."

FEBRUARY 26

I will not be afraid of ten thousands of people, that have set themselves against me round about (Ps. 3:6).

Though a host should encamp against me, my heart shall not fear: though war should rise against me, in this will I be confident (Ps. 27:3).

Thou shalt not be afraid for the terror by night; nor for the arrow that flieth by day (Ps. 91:5).

The Lord is on my side; I will not fear: what can man do unto me? (Ps. 118:6).

Behold, God is my salvation; I will trust, and not be afraid: for the Lord Jehovah is my strength and my song; He also is become my salvation (Isa. 12:2).

GOD'S PROMISE FOR TODAY

When thou liest down, thou shalt not be afraid: yea, thou shalt lie down and thy sleep shall be sweet (Prov. 3:24).

"A rocking horse makes motion, but no progress."

Ye shall not respect persons in judgment; but ye shall hear the small as well as the great; ye shall not be afraid of the face of man; for the judgment is God's: and the cause that is too hard for you, bring it unto me, and I will hear it (Deut. 1:17).

I, even I, am He that comforteth you: who art thou, that thou shouldest be afraid of a man that shall die, and of the son of man which shall be made as grass (Isa. 51:12).

Howbeit no man spake openly of Him for fear of the Jews (John 7:13).

Nevertheless among the chief rulers also many believed on Him; but because of the Pharisees they did not confess Him, lest they should be put out of the synagogue (John 12:42).

GOD'S PROMISE FOR TODAY

The fear of man bringeth a snare: but whoso putteth his trust in the Lord shall be safe (Prov. 29:25).

"Act faith, and it will bring results."

Blessed is the man that heareth me, watching daily at my gates, waiting at the posts of my doors (Prov. 8:34).

The ear that heareth the reproof of life abideth among the wise (Prov. 15:31).

Keep thy foot when thou goest to the house of God, and be more ready to hear, than to give the sacrifice of fools: for they consider not that they do evil (Eccles. 5:1).

But that on the good ground are they, which is an honest and good heart, having heard the word, keep it, and bring forth fruit with patience (Luke 8:15).

Wherefore, my beloved brethren, let every man be swift to hear, slow to speak, slow to wrath (James 1:19).

GOD'S PROMISE FOR TODAY

But be ye doers of the word, and not hearers only, deceiving your own selves (James 1:22).

"Prayer is the key of the morning and bolt of the night."

Notwithstanding, in this rejoice not, that the spirits are subject unto you; but rather rejoice, because your names are written in heaven (Luke 10:20).

In My Father's house are many mansions: if it were not so, I would have told you. I go to prepare a place for you (John 14:2).

For we know that, if our earthly house of this tabernacle were dissolved, we have a building of God, a house not made with hands, eternal in the heavens (II Cor. 5:1).

For he looked for a city which hath foundations, whose builder and maker is God (Heb. 11:10).

Blessed are they that do His commandments, that they may have right to the tree of life, and may enter in through the gates into the city (Rev. 22:14).

GOD'S PROMISE FOR TODAY

But lay up for yourselves treasures in heaven, where neither moth nor rust doth corrupt, and where thieves do not break through nor steal (Matt. 6:20).

"The man who walks with God always gets
to his destination."

March

MARCH 1

He shall deliver thee in six troubles: yea, in seven there shall no evil touch thee (Job 5:19).

Surely He shall deliver thee from the snare of the fowler, and from the noisome pestilence (Ps. 91:3).

There hath no temptation taken you but such as is common to man: but God is faithful, Who will not suffer you to be tempted above that ye are able; but will with the temptation also make a way to escape, that ye may be able to bear it (I Cor. 10:13).

And the Lord shall deliver me from every evil work, and will preserve me unto His heavenly kingdom: to Whom be glory for ever and ever. Amen (II Tim. 4:18).

GOD'S PROMISE FOR TODAY

The Lord knoweth how to deliver the godly out of temptations and to reserve the unjust unto the day of judgment to be punished (II Peter 2:9).

"When doubt calls let faith answer the door."

MARCH 2

And he said, the Lord is my rock and my fortress, and my deliverer (II Sam. 22:2).

And even to your old age I am He; and even to hoar hairs will I carry you: I have made, and I will bear; even I will carry, and will deliver you (Isa. 46:4).

I will love Thee, O Lord, my strength (Ps. 18:1).

He delivereth and rescueth, and He worketh signs and wonders in heaven and in earth, Who hath delivered Daniel from the power of the lions (Dan. 6:27).

Who delivered us from so great a death, and doth deliver: in Whom we trust that He will yet deliver us (II Cor. 1:10).

And deliver them, who through fear of death were all their lifetime subject to bondage (Heb. 2:15).

GOD'S PROMISE FOR TODAY

Be not afraid of their faces: for I am with thee to deliver thee, saith the Lord (Jer. 1:8).

"To lose all for Christ is my best gain; and to gain all without Him would be my worst loss."

MARCH 3

And all Judah rejoiced at the oath: for they had sworn with all their heart, and sought Him with their whole desire; and He was found of them: and the Lord gave them rest round about (II Chron. 15:15).

Lord, all my desire is before Thee; and my groaning is not hid from Thee (Ps. 38:9).

With my soul have I desired Thee in the night; yea, with my spirit within me will I seek Thee early: for when Thy judgments are in the earth, the inhabitants of the world will learn righteousness (Isa. 26:9).

Blessed are ye that hunger now: for ye shall be filled. Blessed are ye that weep now: for ye shall laugh (Luke 6:21).

As newborn babes, desire the sincere milk of the word, that ye may grow thereby (I Peter 2:2).

GOD'S PROMISE FOR TODAY

Whom have I in heaven but Thee? and there is none upon earth that I desire beside Thee (Ps. 73:25).

"Some people are like blotters—soak up everything but get it backwards."

MARCH 4

As for me, I will behold Thy face in righteousness: I shall be satisfied, when I awake, with Thy likeness (Ps. 17:15).

My soul shall be satisfied as with marrow and fatness; and my mouth shall praise Thee with joyful lips (Ps. 63:5).

Who satisfieth thy mouth with good things; so that thy youth is renewed like the eagles' (Ps. 103:5).

And the Lord shall guide thee continually, and satisfy thy soul in drought, and make fat thy bones: and thou shalt be like a watered garden, and like a spring of water, whose waters fail not (Isa. 58:11).

GOD'S PROMISE FOR TODAY

How excellent is Thy lovingkindness, O God! therefore the children of men put their trust under the shadow of Thy wings. They shall be abundantly satisfied with the fatness of Thy house; and Thou shalt make them drink of the river of Thy pleasures. (Ps. 36:7, 8).

"Our responsibility is—response to His ability."

MARCH 5

Ho, every one that thirsteth, come ye to the waters, and he that hath no money; come ye, buy, and eat; yea, come, buy wine and milk without money and without price (Isa. 55:1).

But whosoever drinketh of the water that I shall give him shall never thirst; but the water that I shall give him shall be in him a well of water springing up into everlasting life (John 4:14).

In the last day, that great day of the feast, Jesus stood and cried, saying, If any man thirst, let him come unto Me, and drink (John 7:37).

They shall hunger no more, neither thirst any more; neither shall the sun light on them, nor any heat (Rev. 7:16).

And the Spirit and the bride say, Come. And let him that heareth say, Come. And let him that is athirst come. And whosoever will, let him take the water of life freely (Rev. 22:17).

GOD'S PROMISE FOR TODAY

Blessed are they which do hunger and thirst after righteousness: for they shall be filled (Matt. 5:6).

"A man wrapped up in himself makes a very small package."

MARCH 6

The backslider in heart shall be filled with his own ways: and a good man shall be satisfied from himself (Prov. 14:14).

And because iniquity shall abound, the love of many shall wax cold (Matt. 24:12).

And Jesus said unto him. No man, having put his hand to the plough and looking back, is fit for the kingdom of God (Luke 9:62).

But now, after that ye have known God, or rather are known of God, how turn ye again to the weak and beggarly elements, whereunto ye desire again to be in bondage? (Gal. 4:9).

Nevertheless I have somewhat against thee, because thou has left thy first love (Rev. 2:4).

GOD'S PROMISE FOR TODAY

Now the just shall live by faith: but if any man draw back, My soul shall have no pleasure in him (Heb. 10:38).

" 'Still religion' like still water freezes first."

MARCH 7

But speaking the truth in love, may grow up into Him in all things, which is the head, even Christ (Eph. 4:15).

And the Lord make you to increase and abound in love one toward another, and toward all men, even as we do toward you (I Thess. 3:12).

Therefore leaving the principles of the doctrine of Christ, let us go on unto perfection; not laying again the foundation of repentance from dead works, and of faith toward God (Heb. 6:1).

As newborn babes, desire the sincere milk of the word, that ye may grow thereby (I Peter 2:2).

But grow in grace, and in the knowledge of our Lord and Saviour Jesus Christ. To Him be glory both now and forever (II Peter 3:18).

GOD'S PROMISE FOR TODAY

And this, giving all diligence, add to your faith virtue; and to virtue, knowledge; and to knowledge, temperance; and to temperance, patience; and to patience, godliness (II Peter 1:5, 6).

"Never be yoked to one who refuses the yoke of Christ."

MARCH 8

And the child Samuel grew on, and was in favour both with the Lord, and also with men (I Sam. 2:26).

And the child grew, and waxed strong in spirit, and was in the deserts till the day of his shewing unto Israel (Luke 1:80).

And the child grew, and waxed strong in spirit, filled with wisdom: and the grace of God was upon Him (Luke 2:40).

And Jesus increased in wisdom and stature, and in favor with God and man (Luke 2:52).

But Saul increased the more in strength and confounded the Jews which dwelt at Damascus, proving that this is very Christ (Acts 9:22).

GOD'S PROMISE FOR TODAY

We are bound to thank God always for you, brethren, as it is meet, because that your faith groweth exceedingly, and the charity of every one of you all toward each other aboundeth (II Thess. 1:3).

"Many a preacher is dying by 'Degrees.'"

MARCH 9

When I was a child, I spake as a child, I understood as a child, I thought as a child: but when I became a man, I put away childish things (I Cor. 13:11).

Till we all come in the unity of the faith, and of the knowledge of the Son of God, unto a perfect man, unto the measure of the stature of the fulness of Christ (Eph. 4:13).

But strong meat belongeth to them that are of full age, even those who by reason of use have their senses exercised to discern both good and evil (Heb. 5:14).

I have written unto you, young men, because ye are strong, and the word of God abideth in you, and ye have overcome the wicked one (I John 2:14).

GOD'S PROMISE FOR TODAY

Brethren, be not children in understanding: howbeit in malice be ye children, but in understanding be men (I Cor. 14:20).

"It is possible to disagree and still be agreeable."

MARCH 10

And I, brethren, could not speak unto you as unto spiritual, but as unto carnal, even as unto babes in Christ (I Cor. 3:1).

I have fed you with milk, and not with meat: for hitherto ye were not able to bear it, neither yet now are ye able (I Cor. 3:2).

Now I say, that the heir, as long as he is a child, differeth nothing from a servant, though he be lord of all: But is under tutors and governors until the time appointed of the father.

Even so we, when we were children, were in bondage under the elements of the world (Gal. 4:1-3).

That we henceforth be no more children, tossed to and fro, and carried about with every wind of doctrine, by the sleight of men, and cunning craftiness, whereby they lie in wait to deceive (Eph. 4:14).

GOD'S PROMISE FOR TODAY

For when for the time ye ought to be teachers, ye have need that one teach you again which be the first principles of the oracles of God (Heb. 5:12).

"God hears no more than the heart speaks."

MARCH 11

The righteous also shall hold on his way, and he that hath clean hands shall be stronger and stronger (Job 17:9).

They go from strength to strength, every one of them in Zion appeareth before God (Ps. 84:7).

But the path of the just is as the shining light, that shineth more and more unto the perfect day (Prov. 4:18).

Meditate upon these things; give thyself wholly to them; that thy profiting may appear to all (I Tim. 4:15).

We then that are strong ought to bear the infirmities of the weak, and not to please ourselves (Rom. 15:1).

He shall glorify Me: for He shall receive of Mine, and shall shew it unto you (John 16:14).

GOD'S PROMISE FOR TODAY

The righteous shall flourish like the palm tree: he shall grow like a cedar in Lebanon (Ps. 92:12).

"Make the most of life before the most of life is gone."

MARCH 12

I prevented the dawning of the morning, and cried: I hoped in Thy word (Ps. 119:147).

And she was a widow of about fourscore and four years, which departed not from the temple, but served God with fastings and prayers night and day (Luke 2:37).

A devout man, and one that feared God with all his house, which gave much alms to the people, and prayed to God alway (Acts 10:2).

Night and day praying exceedingly that we might see your

face, and might perfect that which is lacking in your faith (I Thess. 3:10).

Now she that is a widow indeed, and desolate, trusteth in God, and continueth in supplications and prayers night and day (I Tim. 5:5).

GOD'S PROMISE FOR TODAY

My voice shalt Thou hear in the morning, O Lord; in the morning will I direct my prayer unto Thee, and will look up (Ps. 5:3).

"Many prayers go to the dead letter office of heaven for want of sufficient direction."

MARCH 13

Give therefore Thy servant an understanding heart to judge Thy people, that I may discern between good and bad: for who is able to judge this Thy so great a people? (I Kings 3:9).

And shall make him of quick understanding in the fear of the Lord: and he shall not judge after the sight of his eyes, neither reprove after the hearing of his ears (Isa. 11:3).

But the natural man receiveth not the things of the Spirit of God: for they are foolishness unto him, neither can he know them because they are spiritually discerned (I Cor. 2:14).

But strong meat belongeth to them that are of full age, even those who by reason of use have their senses exercised to discern both good and evil (Heb. 5:14).

GOD'S PROMISE FOR TODAY

Hear counsel, and receive instruction, that thou mayest be wise in thy latter end. There are many devices in a man's heart; nevertheless the counsel of the Lord, that shall stand (Prov. 10:20, 21).

"He who will not learn except of himself has a fool for a teacher."

MARCH 14

Then said Jesus unto His disciples, If any man will come after Me, let him deny himself, and take up his cross, and follow Me (Matt. 16:24).

If any man come to Me, and hate not his father, and mother, and wife, and children, and brethren, and sisters, yea, and his own life also, he cannot be My disciple (Luke 14:26).

So likewise, whosoever he be of you that forsaketh not all that he hath, he cannot be My disciple (Luke 14:33).

Then said Jesus to those Jews which believed on Him, if ye continue in My word, then are ye My disciples indeed (John 8:31).

GOD'S PROMISE FOR TODAY

Herein is My Father glorified, that ye bear much fruit; so shall ye be My disciples (John 15:8).

"There is no value in a crop of 'wild oats.' "

MARCH 15

Then shall we know, if we follow on to know the Lord; His going forth is prepared as the morning; and He shall come unto us as the rain, as the latter and former rain unto the earth (Hos. 6:3).

Then spake Jesus again unto them, saying, I am the light of the world: he that followeth Me shall not walk in darkness, but shall have the light of life (John 8:12).

If any man serve Me, let him follow Me; and where I am, there shall also My servant be: if any man serve Me, him will My Father honour (John 12:26).

For even hereunto were ye called: because Christ also suffered for us, leaving us an example, that ye should follow His steps (I Peter 2:21).

GOD'S PROMISE FOR TODAY

My sheep hear My voice, and I know them, and they follow Me (John 10:27).

"If you want to walk with God you must go God's way."

MARCH 16

And Moses said, unto the people, Fear ye not, stand still, and see the salvation of the Lord, which He will shew to you today: for the Egyptians whom ye have seen today, ye shall see them again no more for ever (Exod. 14:13).

And, behold, they brought to Him a man sick of the palsy, lying on a bed: and Jesus seeing their faith said unto the sick of the palsy; Son, be of good cheer; thy sins be forgiven thee (Matt. 9:2).

But straightway Jesus spake unto them, saying, Be of good cheer; it is I; be not afraid (Matt. 14:27).

And Jesus came and touched them, and said, Arise, and be not afraid (Matt. 17:7).

And now I exhort you to be of good cheer; for there shall be no loss of any man's life among you, but of the ship (Acts 27:22).

GOD'S PROMISE FOR TODAY

For I the Lord thy God will hold thy right hand, saying unto thee, fear not; I will help thee (Isa. 41:13).

"Fear is unbelief parading in disguise."

MARCH 17

And Elijah said unto her, Fear not; go and do as thou hast said: but make me thereof a little cake first, and bring it unto me, and after make for thee and for thy son (I Kings 17:13).

Fear thou not; for I am with thee; be not dismayed; for I am thy God: I will strengthen thee; yea, I will help thee; Yea, I will uphold thee with the right hand of my righteousness (Isa. 41:10).

When thou passest through the waters, I will be with thee; and through the rivers, they shall not overflow thee: when thou walkest through the fire, thou shalt not be burned; neither shall the flame kindle upon thee. For I am the Lord thy God, the Holy One of Israel (Isa. 43:2, 3).

But the very hairs of your head are all numbered. Fear ye not therefore, ye are of more value than many sparrows (Matt. 10:30, 31).

GOD'S PROMISE FOR TODAY

Fear not: for I have redeemed thee, I have called thee by thy name; thou are Mine (Isa. 43:1).

"Faith is the soul's intake. Love is the soul's outlet."

MARCH 18

And he said, Come with me, and see my zeal for the Lord. So they made him ride in his chariot (II Kings 10:16).

Therefore when thou doest thine alms, do not sound a trumpet before thee, as the hypocrites do in the synagogues and in the streets, that they may have glory of men. Verily I say unto you, They have their reward (Matt. 6:2).

Moreover when ye fast, be not, as the hypocrites, of a sad countenance: for they disfigure their faces, that they may appear unto men to fast. Verily I say unto you, They have their reward (Matt. 6:16).

But all their works they do for to be seen of men: they

make broad their phylacteries, and enlarge the borders of their garments (Matt. 23:5).

GOD'S PROMISE FOR TODAY

And when thou prayest, thou shalt not be as the hypocrites are, for they love to pray standing in the synagogues and in the corners of the streets, that they may be seen of men. Verily I say unto you, They have their reward (Matt. 6:5).

"The devil is willing for a person to profess Christianity as long as he does not practice it."

MARCH 19

For I was an hungred and ye gave Me meat: I was thirsty, and ye gave Me drink: I was a stranger, and ye took Me in (Matt. 25:35).

Naked, and ye clothed Me; I was sick, and ye visited Me: I was in prison, and ye came unto Me (Matt. 25:36).

I have shewed you all things, how that so labouring ye ought to support the weak, and to remember the words of the Lord Jesus, how He said, it is more blessed to give than to receive (Acts 20:35).

Him that is weak in the faith receive ye, but not to doubtful disputations (Rom. 14:1).

To the weak became I as weak, that I might gain the weak: I am made all things to all men, that I might by all means save some (I Cor. 9:22).

GOD'S PROMISE FOR TODAY

Now we exhort you, brethren, warn them that are unruly, comfort the feebleminded, support the weak, be patient toward all men (I Thess. 5:14).

"Nothing costs so little and goes so far as Christian courtesy."

MARCH 20

Take fast hold of instruction: let her not go: keep her; for she is thy life (Prov. 4:13).

Or let him take hold of My strength, that he may make peace with Me: and he shall make peace with Me (Isa. 27:5).

And he called his ten servants, and delivered them ten pounds, and said unto them, Occupy till I come (Luke 19:13).

And the Spirit and the bride say, Come. And let him that heareth say, Come. And let him that is athirst come. And whosoever will, let him take the water of life freely (Rev. 22:17).

Be ye therefore perfect, even as your Father which is in heaven is perfect (Matt. 5:48).

GOD'S PROMISE FOR TODAY

I will take the cup of salvation, and call upon the name of the Lord (Ps. 116:13).

"The love of heaven makes one heavenly."

MARCH 21

And look that thou make them after their pattern, which was shewed thee in the mount (Exod. 25:40).

For I have given you an example, that ye should do as I have done to you (John 13:15).

And be not conformed to this world: but be ye transformed by the renewing of your mind, that ye may prove what is that good, and acceptable, and perfect will of God (Rom. 12:2).

But we all, with unveiled face beholding as in a mirror the glory of the Lord, are transformed into the same image from glory to glory, even as by the Lord the Spirit (II Cor. 3:18).

GOD'S PROMISE FOR TODAY

As obedient children, not fashioning yourselves according to the former lusts in your ignorance: but as He which hath called you is holy, so be ye holy in all manner of conversation (I Peter 1:14, 15).

"Spiritual blessings are lasting;
worldly pleasures are fleeting."

MARCH 22

And thou shalt love the Lord thy God with all thine heart, and with all thy soul, and with all thy might (Deut. 6:5).

Trust in the Lord with all thine heart; and lean not unto thine own understanding (Prov. 3:5).

And ye shall seek Me and find Me, when ye shall search for Me with all your heart (Jer. 29:13).

Therefore also now, saith the Lord, turn ye even to Me with all your heart, and with fasting, and with weeping, and with mourning (Joel 2:12).

The people that walked in darkness have seen a great light: they that dwell in the land of the shadow of death, upon them hath the light shined (Isa. 9:2).

Blessed are they that keep His testimonies, and that seek Him with the whole heart (Ps. 119:2).

"Christ is not sweet until sin is made bitter to us."

MARCH 23

Then I said, I will not make mention of Him, nor speak any more in His name. But His word was in mine heart as a burning fire shut up in my bones, and I was weary with forbearing, and I could not stay (Jer. 20:9).

The lion hath roared, who will not fear? the Lord God hath spoken, who can but prophesy? (Amos 3:8).

But I have a baptism to be baptized with; and how am I straitened till it be accomplished! (Luke 12:50).

I must work the works of Him that sent me, while it is day: the night cometh, when no man can work (John 9:4).

For though I preach the gospel, I have nothing to glory of: for necessity is laid upon me; yea, woe is unto me, if I preach not the gospel! (I Cor. 9:16).

GOD'S PROMISE FOR TODAY

For we cannot but speak the things which we have seen and heard (Acts 4:20).

"The secret of being a saint, is being a saint in secret."

MARCH 24

Whatsoever thy hand findeth to do, do it with thy might; for there is no work, nor device, nor knowledge, nor wisdom, in the grave, whither thou goest (Eccles. 9:10).

Even so ye, forasmuch as ye are zealous of spiritual gifts, seek that ye may excel to the edifying of the church (I Cor. 14:12).

Wherefore I put thee in remembrance, that thou stir up the gift of God, which is in thee by the putting on of my hands (II Tim. 1:6).

As many as I love, I rebuke and chasten: be zealous therefore, and repent (Rev. 3:19).

GOD'S PROMISE FOR TODAY

Yea, I think it meet, as long as I am in this tabernacle, to stir you up by putting you in remembrance; knowing that shortly I must put off this my tabernacle, even as our Lord Jesus hath shewed me (II Peter 1:13, 14).

"It takes many a tumble to keep us humble."

MARCH 25

So we laboured in the work: and half of them held the spears from the rising of the morning till the stars appeared (Neh. 4:21).

My zeal hath consumed me, because mine enemies have forgotten Thy words (Ps. 119:139).

For Zion's sake will I not hold my peace, and for Jerusalem's sake I will not rest, until the righteousness thereof go forth as brightness, and the salvation thereof as a lamp that burneth (Isa. 62:1).

This man was instructed in the way of the Lord; and being fervent in the spirit, he spake and taught diligently the things of the Lord, knowing only the baptism of John (Acts 18:25).

GOD'S PROMISE FOR TODAY

Return to thine own house, and shew how great things God hath done unto thee. And he went his way, and published throughout the whole city how great things Jesus had done unto him (Luke 8:39).

"Only live fish swim up stream."

MARCH 26

Say not ye, there are yet four months, and then cometh harvest? behold, I say unto you, Lift up your eyes, and look on the fields; for they are white already to harvest (John 4:35).

For I could wish that myself were accursed from Christ for my brethren, my kinsmen according to the flesh (Rom. 9:3).

Brethren, my heart's desire and prayer to God for Israel is, that they might be saved (Rom. 10:1).

If by any means I may provoke to emulation them which are my flesh and might save some of them (Rom. 11:14).

GOD'S PROMISE FOR TODAY

To the weak became I as weak, that I might gain the weak; I am made all things to all men, that I might by all means save some (I Cor. 9:22).

"Act as if expecting to live a hundred years, but could die tomorrow."

Know ye not that they which run in a race run all, but one receiveth the prize? So run, that ye may obtain (I Cor. 9:24).

But covet earnestly the best gifts: and yet shew I unto you a more excellent way (I Cor. 12:31).

Even so ye, forasmuch as ye are zealous of spiritual gifts, seek that ye may excel to the edifying of the church (I Cor. 14:12).

Brethren, I count not myself to have apprehended: but this one thing I do, forgetting those things which are behind, and reaching forth unto those things which are before (Phil. 3:13).

Study to shew thyself approved unto God, a workman that needeth not to be ashamed, rightly dividing the word of truth (II Tim. 2:15).

GOD'S PROMISE FOR TODAY

I press toward the mark for the prize of the high calling of God in Christ Jesus (Phil. 3:14).

"What fruit have ye from those things whereof ye are now ashamed?"

For they have not served Thee in their kingdom, and in Thy great goodness that Thou gavest them, and in the large and fat land which Thou gavest before them, neither turned they from their wicked works (Neh. 9:35).

And every one that heareth these sayings of Mine, and doeth them not, shall be likened unto a foolish man, which built his house upon the sand (Matt. 7:26).

Thou oughtest therefore to have put my money to the exchangers, and then at my coming I should have received mine own with usury (Matt. 25:27).

And that servant, which knew his lord's will, and prepared not himself, neither did according to his will, shall be beaten with many stripes (Luke 12:47).

GOD'S PROMISE FOR TODAY

What doth it profit, my brethren, though a man say he hath faith, and have not works? can faith save him? (James 2:14).

"We can only preach the Christ that we live."

Nevertheless, if thou warn the wicked of his way to turn from it; if he do not turn from his way, he shall die in his iniquity; but thou hast delivered thy soul (Ezek. 33:9).

And they all with one consent began to make excuse. The first said unto him, I have bought a piece of ground, and I must needs go and see it: I pray thee have me excused (Luke 14:18).

For the heart of this people is waxed gross, and their ears are dull of hearing, and their eyes have they closed; lest they should see with their eyes, and hear with their ears, and understand with their heart, and should be converted, and I should heal them (Acts 28:27).

GOD'S PROMISE FOR TODAY

How shall we escape, if we neglect so great salvation; which at the first began to be spoken by the Lord, and was confirmed unto us by them that heard Him (Heb. 2:3).

"A smooth sea never made a skillful mariner."

All things are full of labour; man cannot utter it; the eye is not satisfied with seeing, nor the ear filled with hearing (Eccles. 1:8).

There is one alone, and there is not a second: yea, he hath neither child nor brother: yet is there no end of all his labour; neither is his eye satisfied with riches; neither saith he, for whom do I labour, and bereave my soul of good? This is also vanity, yea, it is a sore travail (Eccles. 4:8).

All the labour of man is for his mouth, and yet the appetite is not filled (Eccles. 6:7).

And when he had spent all, there arose a mighty famine in that land; and he began to be in want (Luke 15:14).

GOD'S PROMISE FOR TODAY

He that loveth silver shall not be satisfied with silver; nor he that loveth abundance with increase: this is also vanity (Eccles. 5:10).

"He who fears God has nothing else to fear."

Thou preparest a table before me in the presence of mine enemies: Thou anointest my head with oil; my cup runneth over (Ps. 23:5).

Bring ye all the tithes into the storehouse, that there may be meat in Mine house, and prove Me now herewith, saith the Lord of hosts, if I will not open you the windows of heaven, and pour you out a blessing, that there shall not be room enough to receive it (Mal. 3:10).

These things have I spoken unto you, that My joy might remain in you, and that your joy might be full (John 15:11).

And to know the love of Christ, which passeth knowledge, that ye might be filled with all the fullness of God (Eph. 3:19).

GOD'S PROMISE FOR TODAY

And be not drunk with wine, wherein is excess; but be filled with the Spirit (Eph. 5:18).

"Jehovah filleth to the brim the vessels faith presents to Him."

April

APRIL 1

And they were all filled with the Holy Ghost, and began to speak with other tongues, as the Spirit gave them utterance (Acts 2:4).

Then Peter, filled with the Holy Ghost, said unto them, Ye rulers of the people and elders of Israel (Acts 4:8).

And when they had prayer, the place was shaken where they were assembled together; and they were all filled with the Holy Ghost, and they spake the word of God with boldness (Acts 4:31).

But he, being full of the Holy Ghost, looked up stedfastly into heaven, and saw the glory of God, and Jesus standing on the right hand of God (Acts 7:55).

For he was a good man, and full of the Holy Ghost and of faith: and much people was added unto the Lord (Acts 11:24).

GOD'S PROMISE FOR TODAY

And the disciples were filled with joy, and with the Holy Ghost (Acts 13:52).

"Unless the vessel is clean, whatever you pour into it turns sour."

APRIL 2

Fret not thyself because of evil doers, neither be thou envious against the workers of iniquity (Ps. 37:1).

Envy thou not the oppressor, and choose none of his ways (Prov. 3:31).

A sound heart is the life of the flesh: but envy the rottenness of the bones (Prov. 14:30).

Let not thine heart envy sinners; but be thou in the fear of the Lord all the day long (Prov. 23:17).

Love suffereth long, and is kind; love envieth not; love vaunteth not itself, is not puffed up (I Cor. 13:4).

GOD'S PROMISE FOR TODAY

Let us not be desirous of vainglory, provoking one another, envying one another (Gal. 5:26).

"There is nothing God will not do through one who does not care to whom the credit goes."

APRIL 3

Because he hath set his love upon Me, therefore will I deliver him: I will set him on high, because he hath known My name (Ps. 91:14).

And they that be wise shall shine as the brightness of the firmament; and they that turn many to righteousness, as the stars for ever and ever (Dan. 12:3).

The Lord God is my strength, and He will make my feet like hinds' feet, and He will make me to walk upon mine high places (Hab. 3:19).

And he said unto him, Well, thou good servant: because thou hast been faithful in a very little, have thou authority over ten cities (Luke 19:17).

Do ye not know that the saints shall judge the world? and if the world shall be judged by you, are ye unworthy to judge the smallest matters? (I Cor. 6:2).

GOD'S PROMISE FOR TODAY

To him that overcometh will I grant to sit with Me in My throne, even as I also overcame, and am set down with My Father in His throne (Rev. 3:21).

"Never throw mud. You may hit your mark, but you will have dirty hands."

APRIL 4

So now it was not you that sent me hither, but God: and He hath made me a father to Pharaoh, and lord of all his house, and a ruler throughout all the land of Egypt (Gen. 45:8).

The Lord maketh poor, and maketh rich: He bringeth low, and lifteth up (I Sam. 2:7).

Now therefore so shalt thou say unto My servant David, thus saith the Lord of hosts, I took thee from the sheepcote, from following the sheep, to be ruler over My people, over Israel (II Sam. 7:8).

And He changeth the times and the seasons: He removeth kings, and setteth up kings: He giveth wisdom unto the wise, and knowledge to them that know understanding (Dan. 2:21).

GOD'S PROMISE FOR TODAY

But God is the judge: He putteth down one, and setteth up another (Ps. 75:7).

"What you laugh at tells plainer than words what you are."

APRIL 5

Then said Jesus unto His disciples, If any man will come after Me, let him deny himself, and take up his cross and follow Me (Matt. 16:24).

For I have given you an example, that ye should do as I have done to you (John 13:15).

Wherefore, holy brethren, partakers of the heavenly calling, consider the Apostle and High Priest of our profession, Christ Jesus (Heb. 3:1).

Looking unto Jesus the author and finisher of our faith, Who for the joy that was set before Him endured the cross, despising the shame, and is set down at the right hand of the throne of God (Heb. 12:2).

For even hereunto were ye called: because Christ also suffered for us, leaving us an example, that ye should follow His steps (I Peter 2:21).

GOD'S PROMISE FOR TODAY

Take my yoke upon you, and learn of Me; for I am meek and lowly in heart: and ye shall find rest unto your souls (Matt. 11:29).

"Wedlock should be a padlock."

APRIL 6

I said, I will take heed to my ways, that I sin not with my tongue: I will keep my mouth with a bridle, while the wicked is before me (Ps. 39:1).

Lay not up for yourselves treasures upon earth, where moth

and rust doth corrupt, and where thieves break through and steal (Matt. 6:19).

And whosoever of you will be the chiefest, shall be servant of all (Mark 10:44).

Casting down imaginations and every high thing that exalteth itself against the knowledge of God, and bringing into captivity every thought to the obedience of Christ (II Cor. 10:5).

Mortify therefore your members which are upon the earth; fornication, uncleanness, inordinate affection, evil concupiscence and covetousness, which is idolatry (Col. 3:5).

GOD'S PROMISE FOR TODAY

Love not the world, neither the things that are in the world. If any man love the world, the love of the Father is not in him (I John 2:15).

"You will never have a friend if you must have one without faults."

APRIL 7

And the apostles said unto the Lord, increase our faith (Luke 17:5).

So then faith cometh by hearing, and hearing by the word of God (Rom. 10:17).

And he that doubteth is damned if he eat, because he eateth not of faith: for whatsoever is not of faith is sin (Rom. 14:23).

For in Jesus Christ neither circumcision availeth anything, nor uncircumcision: but faith which worketh by love (Gal. 5:6).

Now faith is the substance of things hoped for, the evidence of things not seen (Heb. 11:1).

For whatsoever is born of God overcometh the world: and this is the victory that overcometh the world, even our faith (I John 5:4).

GOD'S PROMISE FOR TODAY

Even so faith, if it hath not works, is dead, being alone (James 2:17).

"God desires us to soar like eagles, but many are content to scratch like sparrows."

APRIL 8

Believe in the Lord your God, so shall ye be established: believe His prophets, so shall ye prosper (II Chron. 20:20).

Then said they unto Him, What shall we do, that we might work the works of God? (John 6:28).

Jesus answered and said unto them, This is the work of God, that ye believe on Him Whom He hath sent (John 6:29).

But without faith it is impossible to please Him; for he that cometh to God must believe that He is, and that He is a rewarder of them that diligently seek Him (Heb. 11:6).

If any of you lack wisdom, let him ask of God, that giveth to all men liberally, and upbraideth not; and it shall be given him (James 1:5).

But let him ask in faith, nothing wavering. For he that wavereth is like a wave of the sea driven with the wind and tossed (James 1:6).

GOD'S PROMISE FOR TODAY

Above all, taking the shield of faith, wherewith ye shall be able to quench all the fiery darts of the wicked (Eph. 6:16).

"It is hard to express love with a clinched fist."

APRIL 9

That whosoever believeth in Him should not perish; but have eternal life (John 3:15).

Verily, verily I say unto you, he that heareth My word, and believeth on Him that sent Me, hath everlasting life, and shall not come into condemnation; but is passed from death unto life (John 5:24).

Jesus said unto her, I am the resurrection, and the life: he that believeth in Me, though he were dead, yet shall he live (John 11:25).

I am come a light into the world, that whosoever believeth on Me should not abide in darkness (John 12:46).

That if thou shalt confess with thy mouth the Lord Jesus, and shalt believe in thine heart that God hath raised Him from the dead, thou shalt be saved (Rom. 10:9).

GOD'S PROMISE FOR TODAY

But these are written that ye might believe that Jesus is the Christ, the Son of God; and that believing ye might have life through His name (John 20:31).

"The reason a dog has so many friends is because he wags his tail instead of his tongue."

Trust in the Lord, and do good; so shalt thou dwell in the land, and verily thou shalt be fed (Ps. 37:3).

It is better to trust in the Lord than to put confidence in man (Ps. 118:8).

Trust in the Lord with all thine heart; and lean not unto thine own understanding (Prov. 3:5).

Trust ye in the Lord for ever: for in the Lord Jehovah is everlasting strength (Isa. 26:4).

Who is among you that feareth the Lord, that obeyeth the voice of His servant, that walketh in darkness, and hath no light? let him trust the name of the Lord, and stay upon his God (Isa. 50:10).

GOD'S PROMISE FOR TODAY

Commit thy way unto the Lord; trust also in Him; and he shall bring it to pass (Ps. 37:5).

"Kindness is becoming at any age."

APRIL 11

Oh, how great is Thy goodness, which Thou hast laid up for them that fear Thee; which Thou hast wrought for them that trust in Thee before the sons of men! (Ps. 31:19).

Many sorrows shall be to the wicked: but he that trusteth in the Lord, mercy shall compass him about (Ps. 32:10).

The Lord redeemeth the soul of His servants: and none of them that trust in Him shall be desolate (Ps. 34:22).

The fear of man bringeth a snare; but whoso putteth his trust in the Lord shall be safe (Prov. 29:25).

Thou wilt keep him in perfect peace, whose mind is stayed on Thee; because he trusteth in Thee (Isa. 26:3).

GOD'S PROMISE FOR TODAY

They that trust in the Lord shall be as mount Zion, which cannot be removed, but abideth for ever (Ps. 125:1).

"An easy conscience makes a soft pillow."

APRIL 12

Blessed be the Lord, that hath given rest unto His people Israel, according to all that He promised; there hath not failed one word of all His good promise, which He promised by the hand of Moses His servant (I Kings 8:56).

Thy mercy, O Lord, is in the heavens; and Thy faithfulness reacheth unto the clouds (Ps. 36:5).

I will sing of the mercies of the Lord for ever: with my mouth will I make known Thy faithfulness to all generations (Ps. 89:1).

God is faithful, by Whom ye were called unto the fellowship of His Son Jesus Christ our Lord (I Cor. 1:9).

Wherefore, let them that suffer according to the will of God commit the keeping of their souls to Him in well doing, as unto a faithful Creator (I Peter 4:19).

GOD'S PROMISE FOR TODAY

That by two immutable things, in which it was impossible for God to lie, we might have a strong consolation, who have fled for refuge to lay hold upon the hope set before us (Heb. 6:18).

"Postponed obedience is disobedience"

APRIL 13

Wherefore in all things it behooved Him to be made like unto His brethren, that He might be a merciful and faithful high priest in things pertaining to God, to make reconciliation for the sins of the people (Heb. 2:17).

Let us hold fast the profession of our faith without wavering; (for He is faithful that promised) (Heb. 10:23).

And from Jesus Christ, Who is the faithful witness, and the first begotten of the dead, and the prince of the kings of the earth. Unto Him that loved us, and washed us from our sins in His own blood (Rev. 1:5).

And I saw heaven opened and behold a white horse; and He that sat upon him was called Faithful and True and in righteousness He does judge and make war (Rev. 19:11).

GOD'S PROMISE FOR TODAY

But the Lord is faithful, Who shall stablish you, and keep you from evil (II Thess. 3:3).

"Great minds discuss *ideas;*
Average minds discuss *events;*
Small minds discuss *people.*"

APRIL 14

But now, O Lord, Thou art our Father; we are the clay, and Thou our potter; and we all are the work of Thy hand (Isa. 64:8).

After this manner therefore pray ye: Our Father which art in heaven, Hallowed be Thy name (Matt. 6:9).

If ye then, being evil, know how to give good gifts unto your children, how much more shall your Father which is in heaven give good things to them that ask Him? (Matt. 7:11).

For ye have not received the spirit of bondage again to fear; but ye have received the Spirit of adoption, whereby we cry, Abba, Father (Rom. 8:15).

And if ye call on the Father, Who without respect of persons judgeth according to every man's work, pass the time of your sojourning here in fear (I Peter 1:17).

GOD'S PROMISE FOR TODAY

A father of the fatherless, and a judge of the widows, is God in His holy habitation (Ps. 68:5).

"Worry comes through human interference with the divine plan."

APRIL 15

When a man's ways please the Lord, He maketh even his enemies to be at peace with him (Prov. 16:7).

And lo a voice from heaven, saying, This is My beloved Son, in Whom I am well pleased (Matt. 3:17).

And He that sent Me is with Me: the Father hath not left Me alone; for I do always those things that please Him (John 8:29).

But as we were allowed of God to be put in trust with the gospel, even so we speak; not as pleasing men, but God, which trieth our heart (I Thess. 2:4).

Furthermore then we beseech you brethren, and exhort you by the Lord Jesus, that as ye have received of us how ye ought to walk and to please God, so ye would abound more and more (I Thess. 4:1).

GOD'S PROMISE FOR TODAY

But to do good and to communicate forget not; for with such sacrifices God is well pleased (Heb. 13:16).

"An idle person is the devil's playmate."

APRIL 16

For where two or three are gathered together in My name, there am I in the midst of them (Matt. 18:20).

God is faithful, by Whom ye were called unto the fellowship of His Son Jesus Christ our Lord (I Cor. 1:9).

That which we have seen and heard declare we unto you, that ye also may have fellowship with us; and truly our fellowship is with the Father, and with His Son Jesus Christ (I John 1:3).

Behold, I stand at the door and knock: if any man hear my voice, and open the door, I will come in to him and will sup with him, and he with Me (Rev. 3:20).

GOD'S PROMISE FOR TODAY

Now when they saw the boldness of Peter and John, and perceived that they were unlearned and ignorant men, they marvelled; and they took knowledge of them, that they had been with Jesus (Acts 4:13).

"One with God is a majority."

APRIL 17

I have set the Lord always before me: because He is at my right hand, I shall not be moved (Ps. 16:8).

The Lord is nigh unto all them that call upon Him, to all that call upon Him in truth (Ps. 145:18).

Am I a God at hand, saith the Lord, and not a God afar off? (Jer. 23:23).

That they should seek the Lord, if haply they might feel after Him, and find Him, though He be not far from every one of us (Acts 17:27).

But one thing is needful; and Mary hath chosen that good part, which shall not be taken away from her (Luke 10:42).

GOD'S PROMISE FOR TODAY

The Lord is nigh unto them that are of a broken heart; and saveth such as be of a contrite spirit (Ps. 34:18).

"To err is human . . . to forgive is divine."

APRIL 18

And Saul said, Let us go down after the Philistines by night, and spoil them until the morning light, and let us not leave a man of them. And they said, Do whatsoever seemeth good unto thee. Then said the priest, Let us draw near hither unto God (I Sam. 14:36).

But it is good for me to draw near to God; I have put my trust in the Lord God, that I may declare all Thy works (Ps. 73:28).

For the law made nothing perfect, but the bringing in of a better hope did; by the which we draw nigh unto God (Heb. 7:19).

Let us draw near with a true heart in full assurance of faith, having our hearts sprinkled from an evil conscience, and our bodies washed with pure water (Heb. 10:22).

GOD'S PROMISE FOR TODAY

Draw nigh to God, and He will draw nigh to you. Cleanse your hands ye sinners; and purify your hearts, ye double minded (James 4:8).

"Faults are thick where love is thin."

APRIL 19

Abide in me, and I in you. As the branch cannot bear fruit of itself, except it abide in the vine; no more can ye, except ye abide in me (John 15:4).

I am the vine, ye are the branches. He that abideth in Me, and I in him, the same bringeth forth much fruit; for without Me ye can do nothing (John 15:5).

If a man abide not in Me, he is cast forth as a branch and is withered and men gather them, and cast them into the fire, and they are burned (John 15:6).

If ye keep My commandments, ye shall abide in My love; even as I have kept My Father's commandments, and abide in His love (John 15:10).

He that saith he abideth in Him ought himself also so to walk, even as He walked (I John 2:6).

GOD'S PROMISE FOR TODAY

If ye abide in Me, and My words abide in you, ye shall ask what ye will, and it shall be done unto you (John 15:7).

"Two-thirds of promotion is motion."

APRIL 20

And, behold, I am with thee and will keep thee in all places whither thou goest, and will bring thee again into this land; for I will not leave thee, until I have done that which I have spoken to thee of (Gen. 28:15).

And he said, My presence shall go with thee, and I will give thee rest (Exod. 33:14).

When thou goest out to battle against thine enemies, and seest horses, and chariots, and a people more than thou, be not afraid of them; for the Lord thy God is with thee, which brought thee up out of the land of Egypt (Deut. 20:1).

When thou passest through the waters, I will be with thee: and through the rivers, they shall not overflow thee: when thou walkest through the fire, thou shalt not be burned; neither shall the flame kindle upon thee (Isa. 43:2).

GOD'S PROMISE FOR TODAY

For where two or three are gathered in My name, there am I in the midst of them (Matt. 18:20).

"Nothing is easy to the unwilling."

APRIL 21

Then Jesus said unto them, Verily, verily, I say unto you, Moses gave you not that bread from heaven; but My Father giveth you the true bread from heaven (John 6:32).

For the bread of God is He which cometh down from heaven, and giveth life unto the world (John 6:33).

I am the bread of life (John 6:48).

Your fathers did eat manna in the wilderness, and are dead (John 6:49).

This is the bread which cometh down from heaven, that a man may eat thereof, and not die (John 6:50).

I am the living bread which came down from heaven; if any man eat of this bread, he shall live for ever; and the bread that I will give is My flesh, which I will give for the life of the world (John 6:51).

GOD'S PROMISE FOR TODAY

And Jesus said unto them, I am the bread of life; he that cometh to Me shall never hunger; and he that believeth on Me shall never thirst (John 6:35).

"About the only exercise some folks take is jumping to conclusions."

APRIL 22

Who forgiveth all thine iniquities; Who healeth all thy diseases (Ps. 103:3).

But there is forgiveness with Thee, that Thou mayest be feared (Ps. 130:4).

For if ye forgive men their trespasses, your heavenly Father will also forgive you (Matt. 6:14).

Him hath God exalted with His right hand to be a Prince and a Saviour, for to give repentance to Israel, and forgiveness of sins (Acts 5:31).

Be it known unto you therefore, men and brethren, that through this man is preached unto you the forgiveness of sins (Acts 13:38).

In Whom we have redemption through His blood, the forgiveness of sins, according to the riches of His grace (Eph. 1:7).

GOD'S PROMISE FOR TODAY

If we confess our sins, He is faithful and just to forgive us our sins, and to cleanse us from all unrighteousness (I John 1:9).

"If you cannot make light of your troubles, keep them dark."

APRIL 23

Thine own friend, and thy father's friend, forsake not; neither go into thy brother's house in the day of thy calamity: for better is a neighbour that is near than a brother far off (Prov. 27:10).

Iron sharpeneth iron; so a man sharpeneth the countenance of his friend (Prov. 27:17).

Two are better than one: because they have a good reward for their labour (Eccles. 4:9).

For if they fall, the one will lift up his fellow; but woe to him that is alone when he falleth; for he hath not another to help him up (Eccles. 4:10).

Greater love hath no man than this, that a man lay down his life for his friends (John 15:13).

GOD'S PROMISE FOR TODAY

He that maketh many friends doeth it to his own destruction; but there is a friend that sticketh closer than a brother (Prov. 18:24, RV).

"To speak ill of others is only a roundabout way of bragging on yourself."

APRIL 24

Then they that feared the Lord spake often one to another; and the Lord hearkened, and heard it, and a book of remembrance was written before Him for them that feared the Lord, and that thought upon His name (Mal. 3:16).

And they continued stedfastly in the apostles' doctrine and

fellowship, and in breaking of bread, and in prayers (Acts 2:42).

I thank my God upon every remembrance of you (Phil. 1:3).

For your fellowship in the gospel from the first day until now (Phil. 1:5).

But if we walk in the light, as He is in the light, we have fellowship one with another, and the blood of Jesus Christ His Son, cleanseth us from all sin (I John 1:7).

GOD'S PROMISE FOR TODAY

I am a companion of all them that fear Thee, and of them that keep Thy precepts (Ps. 119:63).

"Sorrow makes us bitter or better."

APRIL 25

Bring forth therefore fruits meet for repentance (Matt. 3:8).

Ye have not chosen Me, but I have chosen you, and ordained you, that ye should go and bring forth fruit, and that your fruit should remain; that whatsoever ye shall ask of the Father in My Name, He may give it you (John 15:16).

Wherefore, my brethren, ye also are become dead to the law by the body of Christ; that ye should be married to another, even to Him Who is raised from the dead, that we should bring forth fruit unto God (Rom. 7:4).

Being filled with the fruits of righteousness, which are by Jesus Christ, unto the glory and praise of God (Phil. 1:11).

GOD'S PROMISE FOR TODAY

That ye might walk worthy of the Lord unto all pleasing, being fruitful in every good work, and increasing in the knowledge of God (Col. 1:10).

"Too many folks are as the wheelbarrow; not much good unless pushed, and very easily upset."

APRIL 26

And he shall be like a tree planted by the rivers of water, that bringeth forth his fruit in his season: his leaf also shall not wither; and whatsoever he doeth shall prosper (Ps. 1:3).

But he that received seed into the good ground is he that heareth the word, and understandeth it; which also beareth fruit, and bringeth forth, some a hundredfold, some sixty, some thirty (Matt. 13:23).

Verily, verily, I say unto you, except a corn of wheat fall into the ground and die, it abideth alone; but if it die, it bringeth forth much fruit (John 12:24).

Every branch in Me that beareth not fruit He taketh away: and every branch that beareth fruit, He purgeth it, that it may bring forth more fruit (John 15:2).

GOD'S PROMISE FOR TODAY

I am the vine, ye are the branches. He that abideth in Me, and I in him, the same bringeth forth much fruit; for without Me ye can do nothing (John 15:5).

"Always keep your head up—but be careful to keep your nose at a friendly level."

APRIL 27

And patience, experience; and experience, hope (Rom. 5:4).

Therefore, as ye abound in everything, in faith, and utterance, and knowledge, and in all diligence, and in your love to us, see that ye abound in this grace also (II Cor. 8:7).

And besides this, giving all diligence, add to your faith virtue; and to virtue, knowledge (II Peter 1:5).

And to knowledge, temperance; and to temperance, patience; and to patience, godliness (II Peter 1:6).

And to godliness, brotherly kindness; and to brotherly kindness, charity (II Peter 1:7).

GOD'S PROMISE FOR TODAY

And not only so, but we glory in tribulations also: knowing that tribulation worketh patience (Rom. 5:3).

"The family altar has altered many a family."

APRIL 28

For as the lightning cometh out of the east, and shineth unto the west; so shall also the coming of the Son of man be (Matt. 24:27).

But of that day and hour knoweth no man, no, not the angels of heaven, but My Father only (Matt. 24:36).

Be ye therefore ready also: for the Son of man cometh at an hour when ye think not (Luke 12:40).

For yourselves know perfectly that the day of the Lord so cometh as a thief in the night (I Thess. 5:2).

Which hope we have as an anchor of the soul, both sure and

stedfast, and which entereth into that within the veil (Heb. 6:19).

GOD'S PROMISE FOR TODAY

Behold, I come as a thief. Blessed is he that watcheth and keepeth his garments, lest he walk naked, and they see his shame (Rev. 16:15).

"When you jump at conclusions you can't always expect a happy landing."

APRIL 29

So that ye come behind in no gift; waiting for the coming of the Lord Jesus Christ (I Cor. 1:7).

And the very God of peace sanctify you wholly; and I pray God your whole spirit and soul and body be preserved blameless unto the coming of our Lord Jesus Christ (I Thess. 5:23).

That thou keep this commandment without spot, unrebukeable, until the appearing of our Lord Jesus Christ (I Tim. 6:14).

Looking for that blessed hope, and the glorious appearing of the great God and our Saviour Jesus Christ (Titus 2:13).

And now, little children, abide in Him; that, when He shall appear, we may have confidence, and not be ashamed before Him at His coming (I John 2:28).

GOD'S PROMISE FOR TODAY

Therefore be ye also ready, for in such an hour as ye think not, the Son of man cometh (Matt. 24:44).

"Nobody raises his own reputation by lowering others."

APRIL 30

I the Lord search the heart, I try the reins, even to give every man according to his ways, and according to the fruit of his doings (Jer. 17:10).

For the Son of man shall come in the glory of His Father with His angels; and then He shall reward every man according to his works (Matt. 16:27).

For we must all appear before the judgment seat of Christ; that every one may receive the things done in his body, according to that he hath done, whether it be good or bad (II Cor. 5:10).

And if ye call on the Father, Who without respect of persons judgeth according to every man's work, pass the time of your sojourning here in fear (I Peter 1:17).

And, behold, I come quickly; and my reward is with me, to give every man according as his work shall be (Rev. 22:12).

GOD'S PROMISE FOR TODAY

Also unto Thee, O Lord, belongeth mercy: for Thou renderest to every man according to his work (Ps: 62:12).

"Be not simply good, be good for something."

May

MAY 1

He will swallow up death in victory; and the Lord God will wipe away tears from off all faces; and the rebuke of His people shall He take away from off all the earth: for the Lord hath spoken it (Isa. 25:8).

The last enemy that shall be destroyed is death (I Cor. 15:26).

So when this corruptible shall have put on incorruption, and this mortal shall have put on immortality, then shall be brought to pass the saying that is written, Death is swallowed up in victory (I Cor. 15:54).

But is now made manifest by the appearing of our Saviour Jesus Christ, Who hath abolished death, and hath brought life and immortality to light through the gospel (II Tim. 1:10).

GOD'S PROMISE FOR TODAY

And God shall wipe away all tears from their eyes; and there shall be no more death, neither sorrow nor crying, neither shall there be any more pain: for the former things are passed away (Rev. 21:4).

"A loose tongue may get its owner in a tight place."

MAY 2

Then shall the righteous shine forth as the sun in the kingdom of their Father. Who hath ears to hear, let him hear (Matt. 13:43).

Who appeared in glory, and spake of His decease which He should accomplish at Jerusalem (Luke 9:31).

And if children, then heirs; heirs of God, and joint heirs with Christ: if so be that we suffer with Him, that we may be also glorified together (Rom. 8:17).

Who shall change our vile body, that it may be fashioned like unto His glorious body, according to the working whereby He is able even to subdue all things unto Himself (Phil. 3:21).

When Christ, Who is our life, shall appear, then shall ye also appear with Him in glory (Col. 3:4).

GOD'S PROMISE FOR TODAY

And there shall be no night there; and they need no candle, neither light of the sun; for the Lord God giveth them light: and they shall reign for ever and ever (Rev. 22:5).

"A switch in time, saves crime."

MAY 3

Thou shalt guide me with Thy counsel, and afterward receive me to glory (Ps. 73:24).

For I reckon that the sufferings of this present time are not worthy to be compared with the glory which shall be revealed in us (Rom. 8:18).

Therefore I endure all things for the elect's sake, that they may also obtain the salvation which is in Christ Jesus with eternal glory (II Tim. 2:10).

The elders which are among you I exhort, who am also an elder, and a witness of the sufferings of Christ, and also a partaker of the glory that shall be revealed (I Peter 5:1).

GOD'S PROMISE FOR TODAY

For our light affliction, which is but for a moment, worketh for us a far more exceeding and eternal weight of glory (II Cor. 4:17).

"A hearse is a poor vehicle in which to ride to church. Why wait for it?"

MAY 4

And Jesus said unto him, Verily I say unto thee, To day shalt thou be with Me in paradise (Luke 23:43).

If any man serve Me, let him follow Me; and where I am there shall also my servant be: if any man serve Me, him will My Father honour (John 12:26).

We are confident, I say, and willing rather to be absent from the Body, and to be present with the Lord (II Cor. 5:8).

For I am in a strait betwixt two, having a desire to depart, and to be with Christ; which is far better (Phil. 1:23).

Then we which are alive and remain shall be caught up together with them in the clouds, to meet the Lord in the air: and so shall we ever be with the Lord (I Thess. 4:17).

GOD'S PROMISE FOR TODAY

And if I go and prepare a place for you, I will come again and receive you unto Myself; that where I am, there ye may be also (John 14:3).

"He who abandons himself to God will never be abandoned by God."

MAY 5

And they that be wise shall shine as the brightness of the firmament; and they that turn many to righteousness, as the stars for ever and ever (Dan. 12:3).

His lord said unto him, Well done, good and faithful servant; thou hast been faithful over a few things, I will make thee ruler over many things; enter thou into the joy of thy lord (Matt. 25:23).

But love ye your enemies, and do good, and lend, hoping for nothing again; and your reward shall be great, and ye shall be the children of the Highest; for He is kind unto the unthankful and to the evil (Luke 6:35).

Knowing that whatsoever good thing any man doeth, the same shall he receive of the Lord, whether he be bond or free (Eph. 6:8).

GOD'S PROMISE FOR TODAY

And whosoever shall give to drink unto one of these little ones a cup of cold water only in the name of a disciple, verily I say unto you, he shall in no wise lose his reward (Matt. 10:42).

"Hell is truth seen too late."

MAY 6

Henceforth there is laid up for me a crown of righteousness, which the Lord, the righteous judge, shall give me in that day; and not to me only, but unto all them also that love His appearing (II Tim. 4:8).

Blessed is the man that endureth temptation: for when he is

tried, he shall receive the crown of life, which the Lord hath promised to them that love Him (James 1:12).

And when the chief Shepherd shall appear, ye shall receive a crown of glory that fadeth not away (I Peter 5:4).

The four and twenty elders fall down before Him that sat on the throne, and worship Him that liveth for ever and ever, and cast their crowns before the throne (Rev. 4:10).

GOD'S PROMISE FOR TODAY

Behold, I come quickly; hold that fast which thou hast, that no man take thy crown (Rev. 3:11).

"A little faith brings a soul to heaven, while great faith brings heaven into the soul."

MAY 7

And many of them that sleep in the dust of the earth shall awake, some to everlasting life, and some to shame and everlasting contempt (Dan. 12:2).

Whose fan is in His hand, and He will throughly purge His floor, and gather His wheat into the garner; but He will burn up the chaff with unquenchable fire (Matt. 3:12).

That he may take part of this ministry and apostleship from which Judas by transgression fell, that he might go to his own place (Acts 1:25).

For when they shall say, Peace and safety; then sudden destruction cometh upon them, as travail upon a woman with child, and they shall not escape (I Thess. 5:3).

GOD'S PROMISE FOR TODAY

He that believeth on the Son hath everlasting life: and he that believeth not the Son shall not see life; but the wrath of God abideth on him (John 3:36).

"When obliged to disagree with others, let us not be disagreeable."

MAY 8

Ye that fear the Lord, praise Him; all ye the seed of Jacob, glorify Him; and fear Him, all ye the seed of Israel (Ps. 22:23).

Herein is My Father glorified, that ye bear much fruit; so shall ye be My disciples (John 15:8).

That ye may with one mind and one mouth glorify God even the Father of our Lord Jesus Christ (Rom. 15:6).

For ye are bought with a price: therefore glorify God in your body, and in your spirit, which are God's (I Cor. 6:20).

Father, I will that they also, whom Thou has given Me, be with Me where I am; that they may behold My glory, which Thou hast given Me: for Thou lovedst Me before the foundation of the world (John 17:24).

GOD'S PROMISE FOR TODAY

Let your light so shine before men, that they may see your good works, and glorify your Father which is in heaven (Matt. 5:16).

"Few love to hear of the sins they love to act."

MAY 9

If thine enemy be hungry, give him bread to eat; and if he be thirsty, give him water to drink (Prov. 25:21).

But I say unto you, Love your enemies, bless them that curse you, do good to them that hate you, and pray for them which despitefully use you, and persecute you (Matt. 5:44).

But I say unto you which hear, Love your enemies, do good to them which hate you (Luke 6:27).

But love ye your enemies, and do good and lend, hoping for nothing again; and your reward shall be great, and ye shall be the children of the Highest: for He is kind unto the unthankful and to the evil (Luke 6:35).

Therefore if thine enemy hunger, feed him; if he thirst, give him drink: for in so doing thou shalt heap coals of fire on his head (Rom. 12:20).

GOD'S PROMISE FOR TODAY

See that none render evil for evil unto any man; but ever follow that which is good, both among yourselves, and to all men (I Thess. 5:15).

"It is a *great* thing to do a *little* thing well."

MAY 10

Good and upright is the Lord: therefore will He teach sinners in the way (Ps. 25:8).

He loveth righteousness and judgment: the earth is full of the goodness of the Lord (Ps. 33:5).

The Lord is good, a strong hold in the day of trouble; and He knoweth them that trust in Him (Nah. 1:7).

And He said unto him, Why callest thou Me good? There is none good but One, that is, God: but if thou wilt enter into life, keep the commandments (Matt. 19:17).

Or despisest thou the riches of His goodness and forbearance and long suffering: not knowing that the goodness of God leadeth thee to repentance? (Rom. 2:4).

GOD'S PROMISE FOR TODAY

O taste and see that the Lord is good: blessed is the man that trusteth in Him (Ps. 34:8).

"Peace rules the day when Christ rules the mind."

MAY 11

And the child grew, and waxed strong in spirit, filled with wisdom; and the grace of God was upon Him (Luke 2:40).

For ye know the grace of our Lord Jesus Christ, that, though He was rich, yet for your sakes He became poor, that ye through His poverty might be rich (II Cor. 8:9).

And He said unto me, My grace is sufficient for thee: for My strength is made perfect in weakness. Most gladly therefore will I rather glory in my infirmities, that the power of Christ may rest upon me (II Cor. 12:9).

He counted me faithful, putting me into the ministry (I Tim. 1:12).

Who was before a blasphemer, and a persecutor, and injurious: but I obtained mercy, because I did it ignorantly in unbelief (I Tim. 1:13).

GOD'S PROMISE FOR TODAY

Thou therefore, my son, be strong in the grace that is in Christ Jesus (II Tim. 2:1).

"Every day is judgment day—use a lot of it."

MAY 12

But we believe that through the grace of the Lord Jesus Christ we shall be saved, even as they (Acts 15:11).

But not as the offence, so also is the free gift: for if through the offence of one many be dead, much more the grace of God, and the gift by grace, which is by one man, Jesus Christ, hath abounded unto many (Rom. 5:15).

And if by grace, then is it no more of works: otherwise grace is no more grace. But if it be of works, then is it no more grace; otherwise work is no more work (Rom. 11:6).

For the grace of God that bringeth salvation hath appeared to all men (Titus 2:11).

That being justified by His grace, we should be made heirs according to the hope of eternal life (Titus 3:7).

GOD'S PROMISE FOR TODAY

Being justified freely by His grace through the redemption that is in Christ Jesus (Rom. 3:24).

"The longer a person carries a grouch the heavier it gets."

MAY 13

Or despisest thou the riches of His goodness and forbearance and longsuffering; not knowing that the goodness of God leadeth thee to repentance? (Rom. 2:4).

In Whom we have redemption through His blood, the forgiveness of sins, according to the riches of His grace (Eph. 1:7).

That in the ages to come He might shew the exceeding riches of His grace, in His kindness toward us, through Christ Jesus (Eph. 2:7).

And the grace of our Lord was exceeding abundant with faith and love which is in Christ Jesus (I Tim. 1:14).

But glory, honour, and peace, to every man that worketh good; to the Jew first, and also the Gentile (Rom. 2:10).

GOD'S PROMISE FOR TODAY

But my God shall supply all your need according to His riches in glory by Christ Jesus (Phil. 4:19).

"The future is as bright as the promises of God."

MAY 14

Sing praises to the Lord, which dwelleth in Zion; declare among the people His doings (Ps. 9:11).

Praise the Lord with harp: sing unto Him with the psaltery and an instrument of ten strings (Ps. 33:2).

Let the people praise Thee: O God; let all the people praise Thee (Ps. 67:3).

Let them give glory unto the Lord, and declare His praise in the islands (Isa. 42:12).

By Him therefore let us offer the sacrifice of praise to God continually, that is, the fruit of our lips, giving thanks to His name (Heb. 13:15).

But ye are a chosen generation, a royal priesthood, a holy nation, a peculiar people; that ye should shew forth the praises of Him Who hath called you out of darkness into His marvellous light (I Peter 2:9).

"A smile is an asset—a grouch is a liability."

MAY 15

When thou hast eaten and art full, then thou shalt bless the Lord Thy God for the good land which He hath given thee (Deut. 8:10).

Enter into His gates with thanksgiving, and into His courts with praise: be thankful unto Him, and bless His name (Ps. 100:4).

And let them sacrifice the sacrifices of thanksgiving, and declare His works with rejoicing (Ps. 107:22).

Giving thanks unto the Father, which hath made us meet to be partakers of the inheritance of the saints in light (Col. 1:12).

In everything give thanks; for this is the will of God in Christ Jesus concerning you (I Thess. 5:18).

GOD'S PROMISE FOR TODAY

And let the peace of God rule in your hearts, to the which also ye are called in one body; and be ye thankful (Col. 3:15).

"If you want your dreams to come true don't oversleep."

MAY 16

He maketh me to lie down in green pastures: He leadeth me beside the still waters (Ps. 23:2).

The meek will He guide in judgment: and the meek will He teach His way (Ps. 25:9).

Thou shalt guide me with Thy counsel, and afterward receive me to glory (Ps. 73:24).

And thine ears shall hear a word behind thee, saying, This is the way, walk ye in it, when ye turn to the right hand, and when ye turn to the left (Isa. 30:21).

Howbeit when He, the Spirit of truth, is come, He will guide you into all truth: for He shall not speak of Himself; but whatsoever He shall hear, that shall He speak: and He will shew you things to come (John 16:13).

For this God is our God for ever and ever: He will be our guide even unto death (Ps. 48:14).

"Every man must live with the man he makes of himself."

MAY 17

And thou shalt remember all the way which the Lord thy God led thee these forty years in the wilderness, to humble thee, and to prove thee, to know what was in thine heart, whether thou wouldest keep His commandments, or no (Deut. 8:2).

As an eagle stirreth up her nest, fluttereth over her young, spreadeth abroad her wings, taketh them, beareth them on her wings (Deut. 32:11).

So the Lord alone did lead him, and there was no strange god with him (Deut. 32:12).

Thou leddest Thy people like a flock by the hand of Moses and Aaron (Ps. 77:20).

If I take the wings of the morning, and dwell in the uttermost parts of the sea: even there shall Thy hand lead me, and Thy right hand shall hold me (Ps. 139:9, 10).

GOD'S PROMISE FOR TODAY

Teach me Thy way, O Lord, and lead me in a plain path, because of mine enemies (Ps. 27:11).

"Embark on no enterprise you cannot submit to the test of prayer."

MAY 18

The Lord is my strength and my shield; my heart trusted in Him, and I am helped: therefore my heart greatly rejoiceth; and with my song will I praise Him (Ps. 28:7).

But I am poor and needy; yet the Lord thinketh upon me: Thou art my help and my deliverer; make no tarrying, O my God (Ps. 40:17).

Fear thou not; for I am with thee: be not dismayed; for I am thy God: I will strengthen thee, yea I will help thee; yea, I will uphold thee with the right hand of My righteousness (Isa. 41:10).

Behold, the Lord God will help me; who is he that shall condemn me? lo, they all shall wax old as a garment; the moth shall eat them up (Isa. 50:9).

So that we may boldly say, The Lord is my helper, and I will not fear what man shall do unto me (Heb. 13:6).

"Marrying is like telephoning, you sometimes get the wrong party. Better be careful!"

MAY 19

Every valley shall be exalted, and every mountain and hill shall be made low: and the crooked shall be made straight, and the rough places plain (Isa. 40:4).

And I will make all My mountains a way, and My highways shall be exalted (Isa. 49:11).

Jesus answered and said unto them, Verily I say unto you, if ye have faith, and doubt not, ye shall not only do this which is done to the fig tree, but also if ye shall say unto this mountain, be thou removed, and be thou cast into the sea; it shall be done (Matt. 21:21).

GOD'S PROMISE FOR TODAY

I will go before thee, and make the crooked places straight; I will break in pieces the gates of brass, and cut in sunder the bars of iron (Isa. 45:2).

"If you want to get up—step down.
If you want to be seen—get out of sight.
If you want to be great—forget yourself."

MAY 20

For I am the Lord that bringeth you up out of the land of Egypt, to be your God; ye shall therefore be holy, for I am holy (Lev. 11:45).

That He would grant unto us, that we being delivered out of the hand of our enemies, might serve Him without fear (Luke 1:74).

In holiness and righteousness before Him, all the days of our life (Luke 1:75).

Having therefore these promises, dearly beloved, let us cleanse ourselves from all filthiness of the flesh and spirit, perfecting holiness in the fear of God (II Cor. 7:1).

Follow peace with all men, and holiness, without which no man shall see the Lord (Heb. 12:14).

Because it is written, Be ye holy; for I am holy (I Peter 1:16).

Seeing then that all these things shall be dissolved, what manner of persons ought ye to be in all holy conversation and godliness? (II Peter 3:11).

"There are three answers to prayer—yes, no, and wait."

MAY 21

And I will put My Spirit within you and cause you to walk in My statutes, and ye shall keep My judgments, and do them (Ezek. 36:27).

Even the Spirit of truth; Whom the world cannot receive, because it seeth Him not, neither knoweth Him: but ye know Him; for He dwelleth with you and shall be in you (John 14:17).

But ye are not in the flesh, but in the Spirit, if so be that the Spirit of God dwell in you. Now if any man have not the Spirit of Christ, he is none of His (Rom. 8:9).

But the anointing which ye have received of Him abideth in you, and ye need not that any man teach you: but as the same anointing teacheth you of all things, and is truth, and is no lie, and even as it hath taught you, ye shall abide in Him (I John 2:27).

GOD'S PROMISE FOR TODAY

Know ye not that ye are the temple of God, and that the Spirit of God dwelleth in you? (I Cor. 3:16).

"If you are a stranger to prayer, you are a stranger to power."

MAY 22

The Spirit itself beareth witness with our spirit, that we are the children of God (Rom. 8:16).

And because ye are sons, God hath sent forth the Spirit of His Son into your hearts, crying, Abba, Father (Gal. 4:6).

And he that keepeth His commandments dwelleth in Him, and He in him. And hereby we know that He abideth in us, by the Spirit which He hath given us (I John 3:24).

This is He that came by water and blood, even Jesus Christ; not by water only, but by water and blood. And it is the Spirit that beareth witness, because the Spirit is truth (I John 5:6).

I say the truth in Christ, I lie not, my conscience also bearing me witness in the Holy Ghost (Rom. 9:1).

Hereby know we that we dwell in Him, and He in us, because He hath given us of His Spirit (I John 4:13).

"When men speak evil of thee, so live that no one will believe them."

MAY 23

Thou gavest also Thy good Spirit to instruct them, and withheldest not Thy manna from their mouth, and gavest them water for their thirst (Neh. 9:20).

For the Holy Ghost shall teach you in the same hour what ye ought to say (Luke 12:12).

Which things also we speak, not in the words which man's wisdom teacheth, but which the Holy Ghost teacheth; comparing spiritual things with spiritual (I Cor. 2:13).

But the anointing which ye have received of Him abideth in you, and ye need not that any man teach you: but as the same anointing teacheth you of all things, and is truth, and is no lie, and even as it hath taught you, ye shall abide in Him (I John 2:27).

GOD'S PROMISE FOR TODAY

But the Comforter, which is the Holy Ghost, Whom the Father will send in My name, He shall teach you all things, and bring all things to your remembrance, whatsoever I have said unto you (John 14:26).

"Christianity is a personal (purse-and-all) religion."

MAY 24

But they rebelled and vexed His Holy Spirit: therefore, He was turned to be their enemy, and He fought against them (Isa. 63:10).

Wherefore I say unto you, all manner of sin and blasphemy shall be forgiven unto men: but the blasphemy against the Holy Ghost shall not be forgiven unto men (Matt. 12:31).

But he that shall blaspheme against the Holy Ghost hath never forgiveness, but is in danger of eternal damnation (Mark 3:29).

But Peter said, Ananias, why hath Satan filled thine heart to lie to the Holy Ghost, and to keep back part of the price of the land? (Acts 5:3).

Quench not the Spirit (I Thess. 5:19).

And grieve not the Holy Spirit of God, whereby ye are sealed unto the day of redemption (Eph. 4:30).

"Truth is not always popular, but it is always right."

MAY 25

Howbeit when He, the Spirit of truth, is come, He will guide you into all truth: for He shall not speak of Himself; but whatsoever He shall hear, that shall He speak: and He will shew you things to come (John 16:13).

While Peter thought on the vision, the Spirit said unto him, Behold, three men seek thee (Acts 10:19).

Arise therefore, and get thee down, and go with them, doubting nothing: for I have sent them (Acts 10:20).

As they ministered to the Lord, and fasted, the Holy Ghost said, Separate me Barnabas and Saul for the work whereunto I have called them (Acts 13:2).

Now when they had gone throughout Phrygia and the region of Galatia, and were forbidden of the Holy Ghost to preach the word in Asia (Acts 16:6).

GOD'S PROMISE FOR TODAY

For as many as are led by the Spirit of God, they are the sons of God (Rom. 8:14).

"A Christian should beware of three things—doubt, dirt, and debt."

MAY 26

It is the Spirit that quickeneth; the flesh profiteth nothing: the words that I speak unto you, they are spirit, and they are life (John 6:63)

But if the Spirit of Him that raised up Jesus from the dead dwell in you, He that raised up Christ from the dead, shall also quicken your mortal bodies by His Spirit that dwelleth in you (Rom. 8:11).

Who also hath made us able ministers of the new testament; not of the letter, but of the spirit; for the letter killeth, but the spirit giveth life (II Cor. 3:6).

GOD'S PROMISE FOR TODAY

For Christ also hath once suffered for sins, the just for the unjust, that He might bring us to God, being put to death in the flesh, but quickened by the Spirit (I Peter 3:18).

"Some persons are like a toy balloon: a pin prick and there is nothing left of them."

MAY 27

Therefore shall a man leave his father and his mother and shall cleave unto his wife: and they shall be one flesh (Gen. 2:24).

But I say unto you, that whosoever shall put away his wife, saving for the cause of fornication, causeth her to commit adultery: and whosoever shall marry her that is divorced committeth adultery (Matt. 5:32).

And unto the married I command, yet not I, but the Lord, Let not the wife depart from her husband (I Cor. 7:10).

But and if she depart, let her remain unmarried, or be reconciled to her husband: and let not the husband put away his wife (I Cor. 7:11).

GOD'S PROMISE FOR TODAY

What therefore God hath joined together, let not man put asunder (Mark 10:9).

"Happiness increases the more you spread it around."

MAY 28

And Adam said, This is now bone of my bones, and flesh of my flesh: she shall be called Woman, because she was taken out of man (Gen. 2:23).

Let thy fountain be blessed: and rejoice with the wife of thy youth (Prov. 5:18).

Live joyfully with the wife whom thou lovest all the days of the life of thy vanity, which He hath given thee under the sun, all the days of thy vanity: for that is thy portion in this life, and in thy labour which thou takest under the sun (Eccles. 9:9).

Husbands, love your wives, even as Christ also loved the church, and gave Himself for it (Eph. 5:25).

Likewise, ye husbands, dwell with them according to knowledge, giving honour unto the wife, as unto the weaker vessel, and as being heirs together of the grace of life; that your prayers be not hindered (I Peter 3:7).

GOD'S PROMISE FOR TODAY

Therefore shall a man leave his father and his mother, and

shall cleave unto his wife: and they shall be one flesh (Gen. 2:24).

"Brooding over one's troubles insures a perfect hatch."

MAY 29

Only take heed to thyself, and keep thy soul diligently, lest thou forget the things which thine eyes have seen, and lest they depart from thy heart all the days of thy life: but teach them thy sons, and thy sons' sons (Deut. 4:9).

And that their children, which have not known any thing, may hear, and learn to fear the Lord your God, as long as ye live in the land whither ye go over Jordan to possess it (Deut. 31:13).

Whom shall He teach knowledge? and whom shall He make to understand doctrine? them that are weaned from the milk, and drawn from the breasts (Isa. 28:9).

So when they had dined, Jesus saith to Simon Peter, Simon, son of Jonas, lovest thou Me more than these? He saith unto Him, Yea, Lord; Thou knowest that I love Thee. He saith unto him, Feed My lambs (John 21:15).

GOD'S PROMISE FOR TODAY

Train up a child in the way he should go: and when he is old, he will not depart from it (Prov. 22:6).

"When a man starts throwing dirt, you know he's losing ground."

MAY 30

The Proverbs of Solomon. A wise son maketh a glad father: but a foolish son is the heaviness of his mother (Prov. 10:1).

The father of the righteous shall greatly rejoice: and he that begetteth a wise child shall have joy of him (Prov. 23:24).

Even a child is known by his doings, whether his work be pure, and whether it be right (Prov. 20:11).

And bring hither the fatted calf, and kill it; and let us eat, and be merry (Luke 15:23).

For this my son was dead, and is alive again; he was lost, and is found. And they began to be merry (Luke 15:24).

Hearken unto thy father that begat thee, and despise not thy mother when she is old (Prov. 23:22).

GOD'S PROMISE FOR TODAY

My son, be wise, and make my heart glad, that I may answer Him that reproacheth me (Prov. 27:11).

"The 'Ideals' of some persons are 'I' deals."

MAY 31

Come, ye children, hearken unto me: I will teach you the fear of the Lord (Ps. 34:11).

Whoso loveth wisdom rejoiceth his father (Prov. 29:3).

A wise son maketh a glad father: but a foolish man despiseth his mother (Prov. 15:20).

For Moses said, Honour thy father and thy mother; and, whoso curseth father or mother, let him die the death (Mark 7:10).

Children, obey your parents in the Lord: for this is right (Eph. 6:1).

Honour thy father and mother; which is the first commandment with promise. That it may be well with thee, and thou mayest live long on the earth (Eph. 6:2, 3).

GOD'S PROMISE FOR TODAY

Remember now thy creator in the days of thy youth, while the evil days come not, nor the years draw nigh, when thou shalt say, I have no pleasure in them (Eccles. 12:1).

"Our fruitage for Christ reveals our rootage in Him."

June

JUNE 1

When my father and my mother forsake me, then the Lord will take me up (Ps. 27:10).

Now therefore hearken unto Me, O ye children: for blessed are they that keep my ways (Prov. 8:32).

He shall feed His flock like a shepherd: He shall gather the lambs with His arm, and carry them in His bosom, and shall gently lead those that are with young (Isa. 40:11).

But when Jesus saw it, He was much displeased, and said unto them, Suffer the little children to come unto Me, and forbid them not; for of such is the kingdom of God (Mark 10:14).

For the promise is unto you, and to your children, and to all that are afar off, even as many as the Lord our God shall call (Acts 2:39).

Honour thy father and mother; which is the first commandment with promise (Eph. 6:2).

GOD'S PROMISE FOR TODAY

I love them that love me; and those that seek me early shall find me (Prov. 8:17).

"Prayerfulness begets carefulness."

JUNE 2

And I have also given thee that which thou has not asked, both riches, and honour: so that there shall not be any among the kings like unto thee all thy days (I Kings 3:13).

A man to whom God hath given riches, wealth, and honour, so

that he wanteth nothing for his soul of all that he desireth, yet God giveth him not power to eat thereof, but a stranger eateth it: this is vanity, and it is an evil disease (Eccles. 6:2).

O thou king, the most high God gave Nebuchadnezzar thy father a kingdom, and majesty, and glory, and honour (Dan. 5:18).

If any man serve Me, let him follow Me; and where I am, there shall also My servant be: if any man serve Me, him will My father honour (John 12:26).

GOD'S PROMISE FOR TODAY

He shall call upon Me, and I will answer him: I will be with him in trouble; I will deliver him, and honour him (Ps. 91:15).

"Many persons believe in God, but do not believe God."

JUNE 3

Length of days is in her right hand; and in her left hand riches and honour (Prov. 3:16).

Riches and honour are with me; yea, durable riches and righteousness (Prov. 8:18).

Poverty and shame shall be to him that refuseth instruction: but he that regardeth reproof shall be honoured (Prov. 13:18).

By humility and the fear of the Lord are riches, and honour and life (Prov. 22:4).

But glory, honour, and peace, to every man that worketh good; to the Jew first, and also to the Gentile (Rom. 2:10).

Wherefore do ye spend money for that which is not bread? and your labour for that which satisfieth not? hearken diligently unto me, and eat ye that which is good, and let your soul delight itself in fatness (Isa. 55:2).

GOD'S PROMISE FOR TODAY

He that followeth after righteousness and mercy findeth life, righteousness, and honour (Prov. 21:21).

"Revenge is a sword that wounds the one who wields it."

JUNE 4

Who against hope believed in hope, that he might become the father of many nations, according to that which was spoken, So shall thy seed be (Rom. 4:18).

For we are saved by hope: but hope that is seen is not hope: for what a man seeth, why doth he yet hope for? (Rom. 8:24).

For whatsoever things were written aforetime were written for our learning, that we through patience and comfort of the Scriptures might have hope (Rom. 15:4).

And now abideth faith, hope, love, these three; but the greatest of these is love (I Cor. 13:13).

And every man that hath this hope in Him purifieth himself, even as He is pure (I John 3:3).

GOD'S PROMISE FOR TODAY

But sanctify the Lord God in your hearts: and be ready always to give an answer to every man that asketh you a reason of the hope that is in you, with meekness and fear (I Peter 3:15).

"Many a man is too busy making a living to make life worth living."

JUNE 5

The wicked is driven away in his wickedness: but the righteous hath hope in his death (Prov. 14:32).

And have hope toward God, which they themselves also allow, that there shall be a resurrection of the dead, both of the just and unjust (Acts 24:15).

For the hope which is laid up for you in heaven, whereof ye heard before in the word of the truth of the gospel (Col. 1:5).

That by two immutable things, in which it was impossible for God to lie, we might have a strong consolation, who have fled for refuge to lay hold upon the hope set before us (Heb. 6:18).

Blessed be the God and Father of our Lord Jesus Christ, which according to His abundant mercy hath begotten us again unto a lively hope by the resurrection of Jesus Christ from the dead (I Peter 1:3).

GOD'S PROMISE FOR TODAY

Looking for that blessed hope, and the glorious appearing of the great God and our Saviour Jesus Christ (Titus 2:13).

"The smallest good deed is better than the grandest good intention."

JUNE 6

Better it is to be of a humble spirit with the lowly, than to divide the spoil with the proud (Prov. 16:19).

A man's pride shall bring him low: but honour shall uphold the humble in spirit (Prov. 29:23).

For thus saith the high and lofty One that inhabiteth eternity, Whose name is Holy; I dwell in the high and holy place, with him also that is of a contrite and humble spirit, to revive the spirit of the humble, and to revive the heart of the contrite ones (Isa. 57:15).

Whosoever therefore shall humble himself as this little child, the same is greatest in the kingdom of heaven (Matt. 18:4).

He hath shewed thee, O man, what is good; and what doth the Lord require of thee, but to do justly, and to love mercy, and to walk humbly with thy God? (Mic. 6:8).

GOD'S PROMISE FOR TODAY

By humility and the fear of the Lord are riches, and honour, and life (Prov. 22:4).

"There are two sides to the gospel—the believing side and the behaving side."

JUNE 7

But when thou art bidden, go and sit down in the lowest room; that when he that bade thee cometh, he may say unto thee, friend, go up higher: then shalt thou have worship in the presence of them that sit at meat with thee (Luke 14:10).

But ye shall not be so: but he that is greatest among you, let him be as the younger; and he that is chief, as he that doth serve (Luke 22:26).

For I say, through the grace given unto me, to every man that is among you, not to think of himself more highly than he ought to think; but to think soberly, according as God hath dealt to every man the measure of faith (Rom. 12:3).

Likewise, ye younger, submit yourselves unto the elder. Yea, all of you be subject one to another, and be clothed with humility: for God resisteth the proud, and giveth grace to the humble (I Peter 5:5).

GOD'S PROMISE FOR TODAY

Humble yourselves in the sight of the Lord, and He shall lift you up (James 4:10).

"Good advice is no better than poor advice, unless you follow it."

JUNE 8

The wicked in his pride doth persecute the poor: let them be taken in the devices that they have imagined (Ps. 10:2).

Therefore pride compasseth them about as a chain; violence covereth them as a garment (Ps. 73:6).

Pride goeth before destruction, and a haughty spirit before a fall (Prov. 16:18).

A high look, and a proud heart, and the plowing of the wicked, is sin (Prov. 21:4).

He that is of a proud heart stirreth up strife; but he that putteth his trust in the Lord shall be made fat (Prov. 28:25).

For all that is in the world, the lust of the flesh, and the lust of the eyes, and the pride of life, is not of the Father, but is of the world (I John 2:16).

GOD'S PROMISE FOR TODAY

When pride cometh, then cometh shame: but with the lowly is wisdom (Prov. 11:2).

"The fast age seems more concerned about speed than direction."

JUNE 9

For the wicked boasteth of his heart's desire, and blesseth the covetous, whom the Lord abhorreth (Ps. 10:3).

They that trust in their wealth, and boast themselves in the multitude of their riches (Ps. 49:6).

None of them can by any means redeem his brother, nor give to God a ransom for him (Ps. 49:7).

Whoso boasteth himself of a false gift is like clouds and wind without rain (Prov. 25:14).

But now, ye rejoice in your boastings: all such rejoicing is evil (James 4:16).

In all labour there is profit: but the talk of the lips tendeth only to penury (Prov. 14:23).

Woe to the rebellious children, saith the Lord, that take counsel, but not of Me; and that cover with a covering, but not of My spirit, that they may add sin to sin (Isa. 30:1).

GOD'S PROMISE FOR TODAY

Boast not thyself of tomorrow; for thou knowest not what a day may bring forth (Prov. 27:1).

"History is His-story."

JUNE 10

Salt is good: but if the salt have lost his saltness, wherewith will ye season it? Have salt in yourselves, and have peace one with another (Mark 9:50).

For what knowest thou, O wife, whether thou shalt save thy husband? or how knowest thou, O man, whether thou shalt save thy wife? (I Cor. 7:16).

For from you sounded out the word of the Lord not only in Macedonia and Achaia, but also in every place your faith to Godward is spread abroad; so that we need not to speak any thing (I Thess. 1:8).

By faith Abel offered unto God a more excellent sacrifice than Cain, by which he obtained witness that he was righteous, God testifying of his gifts: and by it he being dead yet speaketh (Heb. 11:4).

GOD'S PROMISE FOR TODAY

Ye are the salt of the earth: but if the salt have lost his savour, wherewith shall it be salted? it is thenceforth good for nothing, but to be cast out, and to be trodden under foot of men (Matt. 5:13).

"Some people fall for everything and stand for nothing."

JUNE 11

For Thou, O God, hast heard my vows: Thou hast given me the heritage of those that fear Thy name (Ps. 61:5).

Thy testimonies have I taken as a heritage for ever: for they are the rejoicing of my heart (Ps. 119:111).

And now, brethren, I commend you to God, and to the word of His grace, which is able to build you up, and to give you an inheritance among all them which are sanctified (Acts 20:32).

To open their eyes, and to turn them from darkness to light, and from the power of Satan unto God, that they may receive forgiveness of sins, and inheritance among them which are sanctified by faith that is in Me (Acts 26:18).

GOD'S PROMISE FOR TODAY

Giving thanks unto the Father, which hath made us meet to be partakers of the inheritance of the saints in light (Col. 1:12).

"You can learn a lot from the Bible; you can learn still more by practicing it."

JUNE 12

Who shall ascend into the hill of the Lord? or who shall stand in His holy place? (Ps. 24:3).

He that hath clean hands, and a pure heart; who hath not lifted up his soul unto vanity, nor sworn deceitfully (Ps. 24:4).

Blessed are the pure in heart: for they shall see God. (Matt. 5:8).

Now the end of the commandment is love out of a pure heart, and of a good conscience, and of faith unfeigned (I Tim. 1:5).

Lay hands suddenly on no man, neither be partaker of other men's sins: keep thyself pure (I Tim. 5:22).

And every man that striveth for the mastery is temperate in all things. Now they do it to obtain a corruptible crown; but we an incorruptible (I Cor. 9:25).

GOD'S PROMISE FOR TODAY

Seeing ye have purified your souls in obeying the truth through the Spirit unto unfeigned love of the brethren, see that ye love one another with a pure heart fervently (I Peter 1:22).

"There is never the wrong time to do the right thing."

JUNE 13

For then shalt thou lift up thy face without spot; yea, thou shalt be stedfast, and shalt not fear (Job 11:15).

Thou are all fair, my love; there is no spot in thee (Song of Sol. 4:7).

Pure religion and undefiled before God and the Father is this, To visit the fatherless and widows in their affliction and to keep himself unspotted from the world (James 1:27).

Wherefore, beloved, seeing that ye look for such things, be diligent that ye may be found of Him in peace, without spot, and blameless (II Peter 3:14).

And from Jesus Christ, Who is the faithful witness, and the first begotten of the dead, and the prince of the kings of the earth. Unto Him that loved us, and washed us from our sins in His own blood (Rev. 1:5).

GOD'S PROMISE FOR TODAY

That He might present it to Himself a glorious church, not having spot, or wrinkle, or any such thing; but that it should be holy and without blemish (Eph. 5:27).

"Some minds are like concrete—thoroughly mixed and permanently set."

JUNE 14

For mine iniquities are gone over mine head: as a heavy burden they are too heavy for me (Ps. 38:4).

For I acknowledge my transgressions: and my sin is ever before me (Ps. 51:3).

Now when they heard this, they were pricked in their heart, and said unto Peter and to the rest of the apostles, Men and brethren, what shall we do? (Acts 2:37).

And as he reasoned of righteousness, temperance, and judgment to come, Felix trembled, and answered, Go thy way for this time; when I have a convenient season, I will call for thee (Acts 24:25).

For this cause we also, since the day we heard it, do not cease to pray for you, and to desire that ye might be filled with the knowledge of His will in all wisdom and spiritual understanding (Col. 1:9).

GOD'S PROMISE FOR TODAY

When I kept silence, my bones waxed old through my roaring all the day long (Ps. 32:3).

"The Lord's day is firm foundation upon which to built a six-story week."

JUNE 15

But I have prayed for thee, that thy faith fail not: and when thou art converted, strengthen thy brethren (Luke 22:32).

Then said Jesus, Father, forgive them: for they know not what they do. And they parted His raiment, and cast lots (Luke 23:34).

And I will pray the Father, and He shall give you another Comforter, that He may abide with you for ever (John 14:16).

I pray for them: I pray not for the world, but for them which Thou hast given me; for they are Thine (John 17:9).

Who is he that condemneth? It is Christ that died, yea rather, that is risen again, Who is even at the right hand of God, Who also maketh intercession for us (Rom. 8:34).

GOD'S PROMISE FOR TODAY

Wherefore He is able also to save them to the uttermost that come unto God by Him, seeing He ever liveth to make intercession for them (Heb. 7:25).

"Do unto others as though you were the others."

Come now, and let us reason together, saith the Lord: though your sins be as scarlet, they shall be as white as snow; though they be red like crimson, they shall be as wool (Isa. 1:18).

Ho, every one that thirsteth, come ye to the waters, and he that hath no money; come ye, buy, and eat; yea, come, buy wine and milk without money and without price (Isa. 55:1).

Again, he sent forth other servants, saying, Tell them which are bidden, Behold, I have prepared my dinner: my oxen and my fatlings are killed, and all things are ready: come unto the marriage (Matt. 22:4).

And the Spirit and the bride say, Come. And let him that heareth say, Come. And let him that is athirst come. And whosoever will, let him take the water of life freely (Rev. 22:17).

GOD'S PROMISE FOR TODAY

Come unto me, all ye that labour and are heavy laden, and I will give you rest (Matt. 11:28).

"Men are religious naturally,
but are Christians supernaturally."

Look unto Me, and be ye saved, all the ends of the earth: for I am God, and there is none else (Isa. 45:22).

Ho, every one that thirsteth, come ye to the waters, and he that hath no money; come ye, buy, and eat; yea, come buy wine and milk without money and without price (Isa. 55:1).

Go ye therefore into the highways, and as many as ye shall find, bid to the marriage (Matt. 22:9).

In the last day, that great day of the feast, Jesus stood and cried, saying, if any man thirst, let him come unto Me and drink (John 7:37).

For there is no difference between the Jew and the Greek: for the same Lord over all is rich unto all that call upon Him (Rom. 10:12).

And the Spirit and the bride say, Come. And let him that heareth say, Come. And let him that is athirst come. And whosoever will, let him take the water of life freely (Rev. 22:17).

GOD'S PROMISE FOR TODAY

Who will have all men to be saved, and to come unto the knowledge of the truth (I Tim. 2:4).

"Great truths are not caught on the fly."

In that hour Jesus rejoiced in spirit, and said, I thank Thee, O Father, Lord of heaven and earth, that Thou hast hid these things from the wise and prudent, and hast revealed them unto babes: even so, Father, for so it seemed good in Thy sight (Luke 10:21).

And when he hath found it, he layeth it on his shoulders, rejoicing (Luke 15:5).

And now come I to Thee; and these things I speak in the world, that they might have my joy fulfilled in themselves (John 17:13).

Looking unto Jesus the author and finisher of our faith, Who for the joy that was set before Him endured the cross, despising the shame, and is set down at the right hand of the throne of God (Heb. 12:2).

GOD'S PROMISE FOR TODAY

These things have I spoken unto you, that My joy might remain in you and that your joy might be full (John 15:11).

"The church must know her Head in order to go ahead."

JUNE 19

For His anger endureth but a moment; in His favour is life: weeping may endure for a night, but joy cometh in the morning (Ps. 30:5).

They that sow in tears shall reap in joy (Ps. 126:5).

Hitherto have ye asked nothing in My name: ask, and ye shall receive, that your joy may be full (John 16:24).

For the kingdom of God is not meat and drink; but righteousness, and peace, and joy in the Holy Ghost (Rom. 14:17).

For, behold, the day cometh, that shall burn as an oven and all the proud, yea, and all that do wickedly, shall be stubble: and the day that cometh shall burn them up, saith the Lord of hosts, that it shall leave them neither root nor branch (Mal. 4:1).

GOD'S PROMISE FOR TODAY

Thou wilt shew me the path of life: in Thy presence is fulness of joy; at Thy right hand there are pleasures for evermore (Ps. 16:11).

"Many people itch for what they want, but they seldom scratch for it."

And he believed in the Lord; and He counted it to him for righteousness (Gen. 15:6).

And such were some of you: but ye are washed, but ye are sanctified, but ye are justified in the name of the Lord Jesus, and by the Spirit of our God (I Cor. 6:11).

And such were some of you: but ye are washed, ye are sanctified, but ye are justified in the name of the Lord Jesus, and by the Spirit of our God (I Cor. 6:11).

In Him was life; and the life was the light of men (John 1:4).

Wherefore the law was our schoolmaster to bring us unto Christ, that we might be justified by faith (Gal. 3:24).

Not by works of righteousness which we have done, but according to His mercy He saved us, by the washing of regeneration, and renewing of the Holy Ghost (Titus 3:5).

GOD'S PROMISE FOR TODAY

Therefore being justified by faith, we have peace with God through our Lord Jesus Christ (Rom. 5:1).

"The rest of your days depends on the rest of your nights."

Be kindly affectioned one to another with brotherly love; in honour preferring one another (Rom. 12:10).

Love suffereth long, and is kind; love envieth not: love vaunteth not itself, is not puffed up (I Cor. 13:4).

Put on therefore, as the elect of God, holy and beloved, bowels of mercies, kindness, humbleness of mind, meekness, long-suffering (Col. 3:12).

And besides this, giving all diligence, add to your faith virtue; and to virtue knowledge (II Peter 1:5).

And to knowledge, temperance; and to temperance, patience; and to patience, godliness (II Peter 1:6).

And to godliness, brotherly kindness; and to brotherly kindness, love (II Peter 1:7).

GOD'S PROMISE FOR TODAY

And be ye kind one to another, tender-hearted, forgiving one another, even as God for Christ's sake, hath forgiven you (Eph. 4:32).

"Whether it's on the road or in an argument, when the color changes to red, Stop!"

Yea, if thou criest after knowledge, and liftest up thy voice for understanding (Prov. 2:3).

If thou seekest her as silver, and searchest for her as for hid treasures (Prov. 2:4).

Then shalt thou understand the fear of the Lord, and find the knowledge of God (Prov. 2:5).

Get wisdom, get understanding: forget it not; neither decline from the words of My mouth (Prov. 4:5).

The heart of him that hath understanding seeketh knowledge: but the mouth of fools feedeth on foolishness (Prov. 15:14).

Buy the truth, and sell it not; also wisdom, and instruction, and understanding (Prov. 23:23).

And besides this, giving all diligence, add to your faith virtue; and to virtue, knowledge (II Peter 1:5).

GOD'S PROMISE FOR TODAY

Happy is the man that findeth wisdom, and the man that getteth understanding (Prov. 3:13).

"The man who is always finding fault, seldom finds anything else."

For I know that my Redeemer liveth, and that He shall stand at the latter day upon the earth (Job 19:25).

For we know that, if our earthly house of this tabernacle were dissolved, we have a building of God, a house not made with hands, eternal in the heavens (II Cor. 5:1).

For the which cause I also suffer these things: nevertheless I am not ashamed; for I know Whom I have believed, and am persuaded that He is able to keep that which I have committed unto Him against that day (II Tim. 1:12).

Beloved, now are we the sons of God, and it doth not yet appear what we shall be: but we know that, when He shall appear, we shall be like Him; for we shall see Him as He is (I John 3:2).

GOD'S PROMISE FOR TODAY

And we know that all things work together for good to them that love God, to them who are the called according to His purpose (Rom. 8:28).

"Why envy rich people? They are only poor people with money."

The Lord is good, a strong hold in the day of trouble; and He knoweth them that trust in Him (Nah. 1:7).

Nathanael saith unto Him, Whence knowest Thou me? Jesus answered and said unto him, Before that Philip called thee, when thou wast under the fig tree, I saw thee (John 1:48).

To him the porter openeth; and the sheep hear his voice; and he calleth his own sheep by name, and leadeth them out (John 10:3).

I am the Good Shepherd, and know My sheep, and am known of Mine (John 10:14).

Nevertheless the foundation of God standeth sure, having this seal, The Lord knoweth them that are His. And, let every one that nameth the name of Christ depart from iniquity (II Tim. 2:19).

GOD'S PROMISE FOR TODAY

But if any man love God, the same is known of Him (I Cor. 8:3).

"If you have an half hour to spare don't spend it with someone who hasn't."

In that day, saith the Lord of hosts, will I take thee, O Zerubbabel, My servant, the son of Shealtiel, saith the Lord, and will make thee as a signet: for I have chosen thee, saith the Lord of hosts (Hag. 2:23).

Ye have not chosen Me, but I have chosen you, and ordained you, that ye should go and bring forth fruit, and that your fruit should remain: that whatsoever ye shall ask of the Father in My name, He may give it you (John 15:16).

But the Lord said unto him, Go thy way: for he is a chosen vessel unto Me, to bear My name before the Gentiles, and kings, and the children of Israel (Acts 9:15).

That no flesh should glory in His presence (I Cor. 1:29).

GOD'S PROMISE FOR TODAY

But God hath chosen the foolish things of the world to confound the wise: and God hath chosen the weak things of the world to confound the things which are mighty (I Cor. 1:27).

"Our responsibility is our ability to respond."

He that hath a bountiful eye shall be blessed; for he giveth of his bread to the poor (Prov. 22:9).

Bring ye all the tithes into the storehouse, that there may be meat in Mine house, and prove Me now herewith, saith the Lord of hosts, if I will not open you the windows of heaven, and pour you out a blessing, that there shall not be room enough to receive it (Mal. 3:10).

Give, and it shall be given unto you; good measure, pressed down, and shaken together, and running over, shall men give into your bosom. For with the same measure that ye mete withal it shall be measured to you again (Luke 6:38).

But this I say, he which soweth sparingly shall reap also sparingly; and he which soweth bountifully shall reap also bountifully (II Cor. 9:6).

GOD'S PROMISE FOR TODAY

The liberal soul shall be made fat: and he that watereth shall be watered also himself (Prov. 11:25).

"Experience is the best schoolmaster, but the fees are heavy."

But when thou doest alms, let not thy left hand know what thy right hand doeth (Matt. 6:3).

Heal the sick, cleanse the lepers, raise the dead, cast out devils: freely ye have received, freely give (Matt. 10:8).

Or he that exhorteth, on exhortation: he that giveth, let him do it with simplicity: he that ruleth, with diligence: he that sheweth mercy, with cheerfulness (Rom. 12:8).

Upon the first day of the week let every one of you lay by him in store, as God hath prospered him, that there be no gatherings when I come (I Cor. 16:2).

Every man according as he purposeth in his heart, so let him give; not grudgingly, or of necessity; for God loveth a cheerful giver (II Cor. 9:7).

GOD'S PROMISE FOR TODAY

Every man shall give as he is able, according to the blessings of the Lord thy God which he hath given thee (Deut. 16:17).

"The devil is never too busy to rock the cradle of a sleeping saint."

JUNE 28

He that is greedy of gain troubleth his own house; but he that hateth gifts shall live (Prov. 15:27).

As the partridge sitteth on eggs, and hatcheth them not; so he that getteth riches, and not by right, shall leave them in the midst of his days, and at his end shall be a fool (Jer. 17:11).

For the love of money is the root of all evil; which while some coveted after, they have erred from the faith, and pierced themselves through with many sorrows (I Tim. 6:10).

Your gold and silver is cankered: and the rust of them shall be a witness against you, and shall eat your flesh as it were fire. Ye have heaped treasure together for the last days (James 5:3).

GOD'S PROMISE FOR TODAY

He that loveth silver shall not be satisfied with silver; nor he that loveth abundance with increase: this is also vanity (Eccles. 5:10).

"Pride is like a man's shirt—it is the first thing on, and the last thing off."

JUNE 29

The Spirit of the Lord God is upon me; because the Lord hath anointed me to preach good tidings unto the meek; He hath sent me to bind up the broken hearted, to proclaim liberty to the captives, and the opening of the prison to them that are bound (Isa. 61:1).

And ye shall know the truth, and the truth shall make you free (John 8:32).

For the law of the Spirit of life in Christ Jesus hath made me free from the law of sin and death (Rom. 8:2).

Because the creature itself also shall be delivered from the bondage of corruption into the glorious liberty of the children of God (Rom. 8:21).

Therefore with joy shall ye draw water out of the wells of salvation (Isa. 12:3).

GOD'S PROMISE FOR TODAY

Now the Lord is that Spirit: and where the Spirit of the Lord is, there is liberty (II Cor. 3:17).

"The world is better or worse for every man who has lived in it."

A new heart also will I give you, and a new spirit will I put within you: and I will take away the stony heart out of your flesh, and I will give you a heart of flesh (Ezek. 36:26).

Which were born, not of blood, nor of the will of the flesh, nor of the will of man, but of God (John 1:13).

Therefore if any man be in Christ, he is a new creature: old things are passed away; behold, all things are become new (II Cor. 5:17).

Being born again, not of corruptible seed, but of incorruptible, by the word of God, which liveth and abideth for ever (I Peter 1:23).

Whosoever believeth that Jesus is the Christ is born of God: and every one that loveth Him that begat loveth Him also that is begotten of Him (I John 5:1).

GOD'S PROMISE FOR TODAY

Jesus answered and said unto him, Verily, verily, I say unto thee, except a man be born again, he cannot see the kingdom of God (John 3:3).

"Two marks of a Christian—giving and forgiving."

July

JULY 1

For we must needs die, and are as water spilt on the ground, which cannot be gathered up again; neither doth God respect any person; yet doth He devise means, that His banished be not expelled from Him (II Sam. 14:14).

For he seeth that wise men die, likewise, the fool and the brutish person perish, and leave their wealth to others (Ps. 49:10).

There is no man that hath power over the spirit to retain the spirit; neither hath he power in the day of death: and there is no discharge in that war; neither shall wickedness deliver those that are given to it (Eccles. 8:8).

Wherefore, as by one man sin entered into the world, and death by sin; and so death passed upon all men, for that all have sinned (Rom. 5:12).

GOD'S PROMISE FOR TODAY

And as it is appointed unto men once to die, but after this the judgment (Heb. 9:27).

"Before criticizing another's faults, take time to count ten— of your own."

JULY 2

Yea, though I walk through the valley of the shadow of death, I will fear no evil; for Thou art with me; Thy rod and Thy staff they comfort me (Ps. 23:4).

The wicked is driven away in his wickedness: but the righteous hath hope in his death (Prov. 14:32).

For whether we live, we live unto the Lord; and whether we die, we die unto the Lord: whether we live therefore, or die, we are the Lord's (Rom. 14:8).

For to me to live is Christ, and to die is gain (Phil. 1:21).

And I heard a voice from heaven saying unto me, Write, blessed are the dead which die in the Lord from henceforth: Yea, saith the Spirit, that they may rest from their labours; and their works do follow them (Rev. 14:13).

For I know that Thou wilt bring me to death, and to the house appointed for all living (Job 30:23).

GOD'S PROMISE FOR TODAY

Precious in the sight of the Lord is the death of His saints (Ps. 116:15).

"Even a woodpecker owes his success to the fact that he uses his head."

JULY 3

So let all Thine enemies perish, O Lord: but let them that love Him be as the sun when he goeth forth in his might (Judg. 5:31).

For so hath the Lord commanded us, saying, I have set thee to be a light of the Gentiles, that thou shouldest be for salvation unto the ends of the earth (Acts 13:47).

For ye were sometime darkness, but now are ye light in the Lord: walk as children of light (Eph. 5:8).

That ye may be blameless and harmless, the sons of God, without rebuke, in the midst of a crooked and perverse nation, among whom ye shine as lights in the world (Phil. 2:15).

To give light to them that sit in darkness and in the shadow of death, to guide our feet into the way of peace (Luke 1:79).

GOD'S PROMISE FOR TODAY

Ye are the light of the world. A city that is set on a hill cannot be hid (Matt. 5:14).

"Men are born with two eyes, but only one tongue, that they may see twice as much as they speak."

JULY 4

Then Jesus said unto him, Yet a little while is the light with you. Walk while ye have the light, lest darkness come upon you: for he that walketh in darkness knoweth not whither he goeth (John 12:35).

For God, Who commanded the light to shine out of darkness, hath shined in our hearts, to give the light of the knowledge of the glory of God in the face of Jesus Christ (II Cor. 4:6).

Wherefore, He saith, Awake thou that sleepest, and arise from the dead, and Christ shall give thee light (Eph. 5:14).

And the city had no need of the sun, neither of the moon, to shine in it: for the glory of God did lighten it, and the Lamb is the light thereof (Rev. 21:23).

GOD'S PROMISE FOR TODAY

Then spake Jesus again unto them, saying, I am the light of the world: he that followeth Me shall not walk in darkness, but shall have the light of life (John 8:12).

"The cause, not the pain, makes a martyr."

JULY 5

The Lord is my light and my salvation; whom shall I fear? The Lord is the strength of my life; of whom shall I be afraid? (Ps. 27:1).

Thy sun shall no more go down; neither shall thy moon withdraw itself: for the Lord shall be thine everlasting light, and the days of thy mourning shall be ended (Isa. 60:20).

This then is the message which we have heard of Him, and declare unto you, that God is light, and in Him is no darkness at all (I John 1:5).

And there shall be no night there; and they need no candle, neither light of the sun; for the Lord God giveth them light: and they shall reign for ever and ever (Rev. 22:5).

GOD'S PROMISE FOR TODAY

For the Lord God is a sun and shield: the Lord will give grace and glory: no good thing will He withhold from them that walk uprightly (Ps. 84:11).

"The man who is waiting for something to turn up might do well to start with his own shirt sleeves."

JULY 6

The watchman said, The morning cometh, and also the night: if ye will inquire, inquire ye: return, come (Isa. 21:12).

Arise, shine; for thy light is come, and the glory of the Lord is risen upon thee (Isa. 60:1).

But unto you that fear My name shall the Sun of righteousness arise with healing in His wings; and ye shall go forth, and grow up as calves of the stall (Mal. 4:2).

Through the tender mercy of our God; whereby the dayspring from on high hath visited us (Luke 1:78).

We have also a more sure word of prophecy; whereunto ye do well that ye take heed, as unto a light that shineth in a dark place, until the day dawn, and the day star arise in your hearts (II Peter 1:19).

GOD'S PROMISE FOR TODAY

The night is far spent, the day is at hand: let us therefore cast off the works of darkness, and let us put on the armour of light (Rom. 13:12).

"A God-forsaken man is a man who has forsaken God."

JULY 7

And thou shalt go to thy fathers in peace; thou shalt be buried in a good old age (Gen. 15:15).

Cast me not off in the time of old age; forsake me not when my strength faileth (Ps. 71:9).

Remember now thy Creator in the days of thy youth, while the evil days come not, nor the years draw nigh, when thou shalt say, I have no pleasure in them (Eccles. 12:1).

And even to your old age I am He; and even to hoar hairs will I carry you: I have made, and I will bear; even I will carry, and will deliver you (Isa. 46:4).

That the aged men be sober, grave, temperate, sound in faith, in charity, in patience. The aged women likewise, that they be in behaviour as becometh holiness, not false accusers, not given to much wine, teachers of good things (Titus 2:2, 3).

GOD'S PROMISE FOR TODAY

The hoary head is a crown of glory, if it be found in the way of righteousness (Prov. 16:31).

"Success is 10 percent inspiration and
90 percent perspiration

JULY 8

Love ye therefore the stranger: for ye were strangers in the land of Egypt (Deut. 10:19).

Thou shalt love thy neighbour as thyself (Matt. 22:39).

This is My commandment, that ye love one another, as I have loved you (John 15:12).

Let love be without dissimulation. Abhor that which is evil; cleave to that which is good (Rom. 12:9).

And the Lord make you to increase and abound in love one toward another, and toward all men, even as we do toward you (I Thess. 3:12).

Seeing ye have purified your souls in obeying the truth through the Spirit unto unfeigned love of the brethren, see that ye love one another with a pure heart fervently (I Peter 1:22).

GOD'S PROMISE FOR TODAY

By this shall all men know that ye are My disciples, if ye have love one to another (John 13:35).

"Walk softly, speak tenderly, pray fervently."

JULY 9

For the love of Christ constraineth us: because we thus judge that if one died for all, then were all dead (II Cor. 5:14).

As the Father hath loved Me, so have I loved you: continue ye in My love (John 15:9).

Greater love hath no man than this, that a man lay down his life for his friends (John 15:13).

Who shall separate us from the love of Christ? shall tribulation, or distress, or persecution, or famine, or nakedness, or peril, or sword? (Rom. 8:35).

Hereby perceive we the love of God, because He laid down His life for us: and we ought to lay down our lives for the brethren (I John 3:16).

GOD'S PROMISE FOR TODAY

I am crucified with Christ: nevertheless I live; yet not I, but Christ liveth in me: and the life which I now live in the flesh I live by the faith of the Son of God, Who loved me, and gave Himself for me (Gal. 2:20).

"Flattery is soft soap—and soft soap is 90 percent 'lie.'"

JULY 10

If ye love Me, keep My commandments. And I will pray the Father, and He shall give you another Comforter, that He may abide with you for ever (John 14:15, 16).

Judas saith unto Him, not Iscariot, Lord, how is it that Thou wilt manifest Thyself unto us, and not unto the world? Jesus answered and said unto him, if a man love Me, he will keep My words: and My Father will love him, and We will come unto him, and make Our abode with him (John 14:22, 23).

For the Father Himself loveth you, because ye have loved Me, and have believed that I came out from God (John 16:27).

Whom having not seen, ye love; in whom, though now ye see Him not, yet believing ye rejoice with joy unspeakable and full of glory (I Peter 1:8).

GOD'S PROMISE FOR TODAY

Grace be with all them that love our Lord Jesus Christ in sincerity. Amen (Eph. 6:24).

"Trust like a child and work like a man."

JULY 11

But the fruit of the Spirit is love, joy, peace, longsuffering, gentleness, goodness, faith (Gal. 5:22).

That Christ may dwell in your hearts by faith; that ye, being rooted and grounded in love, may be able to comprehend with all saints what is the breadth, and length, and depth, and height; And to know the love of Christ, which passeth knowledge (Eph. 3:17, 18, 19).

And walk in love, as Christ also hath loved us, and hath given Himself for us an offering and a sacrifice to God for a sweet-smelling savour (Eph. 5:2).

And above all these things put on love, which is the bond of perfectness (Col. 3:14, RV).

And we have known and believed the love that God hath to us. God is love; and he that dwelleth in love dwelleth in God, and God in him (I John 4:16).

GOD'S PROMISE FOR TODAY

For in Jesus Christ neither circumcision availeth anything, nor uncircumcision; but faith which worketh by love (Gal. 5:6).

"Knowledge and timber shouldn't be much used 'til they are seasoned."

JULY 12

For God so loved the world, that He gave His only begotten Son, that whosoever believeth in Him should not perish, but have everlasting life (John 3:16).

Forasmuch as ye know that ye were not redeemed with corruptible things, as silver and gold, from your vain conversation received by tradition from your fathers; But with the precious blood of Christ, as of a lamb without blemish and without spot (I Peter 1:18, 19).

And from Jesus Christ, Who is the faithful witness, and the first begotten of the dead, and the prince of the kings of the earth. Unto Him that loved us, and washed us from our sins in His own blood (Rev. 1:5).

GOD'S PROMISE FOR TODAY

For ye are bought with a price: therefore glorify God in your body, and in your spirit, which are God's (I Cor. 6:20).

"True prayer is God the Holy Spirit talking to God the Father, in the name of God the Son, and the believer's heart is the prayer-room."

JULY 13

Thou shalt not avenge, nor bear any grudge against the children of thy people, but thou shalt love thy neighbour as thyself: I am the Lord (Lev. 19:18).

Say not thou, I will recompense evil; but wait on the Lord, and He shall save thee (Prov. 20:22).

Say not, I will do so to him as he hath done to me: I will render to the man according to his work (Prov. 24:29).

But I say unto you, that ye resist not evil: but whosoever shall smite thee on thy right cheek, turn to him the other also (Matt. 5:39).

Not rendering evil for evil, or railing for railing: but contrariwise blessing; knowing that ye are thereunto called, that ye should inherit a blessing (I Peter 3:9).

GOD'S PROMISE FOR TODAY

Recompense to no man evil for evil. Provide things honest in the sight of all men (Rom. 12:17).

"A single-track mind is all right if it is on the right track."

JULY 14

But the mercy of the Lord is from everlasting to everlasting upon them that fear Him, and His righteousness unto children's children (Ps. 103:17).

It is of the Lord's mercies that we are not consumed, because

His compassions fail not. They are new every morning (Lam. 3:22, 23).

And rend your heart, and not your garments, and turn unto the Lord your God: for He is gracious and merciful, slow to anger, and of great kindness, and repenteth Him of the evil (Joel 2:13).

Who is a God like unto Thee, that pardoneth iniquity, and passeth by the transgression of the remnant of His heritage? He retaineth not His anger for ever, because he delighteth in mercy (Mic. 7:18).

GOD'S PROMISE FOR TODAY

Not by works of righteousness which we have done, but according to His mercy He saved us, by the washing of regeneration, and renewing of the Holy Ghost (Titus 3:5).

"A praying man can never be a useless man."

JULY 15

The Lord knoweth the thoughts of man, that they are vanity (Ps. 94:11).

For as he thinketh in his heart, so is he: eat and drink, saith he to thee; but his heart is not with thee (Prov. 23:7).

The thought of foolishness is sin: and the scorner is an abomination to men (Prov. 24:9).

O Jerusalem, wash thine heart from wickedness, that thou mayest be saved. How long shall thy vain thoughts lodge within thee? (Jer. 4:14).

And Jesus knowing their thoughts said, wherefore think ye evil in your hearts? (Matt. 9:4).

For out of the heart proceed evil thoughts, murders, adulteries, fornications, thefts, false witness, blasphemies (Matt. 15:19).

GOD'S PROMISE FOR TODAY

The thoughts of the wicked are an abomination to the Lord: but the words of the pure are pleasant words (Prov. 15:26).

"The unspeakable gift calls for spoken gratitude."

JULY 16

We have thought of Thy lovingkindness, O God, in the midst of Thy temple (Ps. 48:9).

I thought on my ways, and turned my feet unto Thy testimonies (Ps. 119:59).

For I say, through the grace given unto me, to every man that is among you, not to think of himself more highly than he ought to think; but to think soberly, according as God hath dealt to every man the measure of faith (Rom. 12:3).

Finally, brethren, whatsoever things are true, whatsoever things are honest, whatsoever things are just, whatsoever things are pure, whatsoever things are lovely, whatsoever things are of good report; if there be any virtue, and if there be any praise, think on these things (Phil. 4:8).

GOD'S PROMISE FOR TODAY

The thoughts of the righteous are right: but the counsels of the wicked are deceit (Prov. 12:5).

"God gives by promise that we may take by faith."

JULY 17

How much less in them that dwell in houses of clay, whose foundation is in the dust, which are crushed before the moth? (Job 4:19).

Remember, I beseech thee, that Thou hast made me as the clay; and wilt Thou bring me into dust again? (Job 10:9).

What man is he that liveth, and shall not see death? shall he deliver his soul from the hand of the grave? (Ps. 89:48).

But we have this treasure in earthen vessels, that the excellency of the power may be of God, and not of us (II Cor. 4:7).

For we that are in this tabernacle do groan, being burdened: not for that we would be unclothed, but clothed upon, that mortality might be swallowed up of life (II Cor. 5:4).

And as it is appointed unto men once to die, but after this the judgment (Heb. 9:27).

GOD'S PROMISE FOR TODAY

All go unto one place; all are of the dust, and all turn to dust again (Eccles. 3:20).

"Love never asks, 'How much must I do?' but, 'How much can I do?'"

JULY 18

Thou carriest them away as with a flood; they are as a sleep: in the morning they are like grass which groweth up. In the morning it flourisheth and groweth up; in the evening it is cut down and withereth (Ps. 90:5, 6).

The voice said, Cry, and he said, what shall I cry? All flesh is grass, and all the goodliness thereof is as the flower of the field: the grass withereth, the flower fadeth (Isa. 40:6, 7).

I, even I, am He that comforteth you: who art thou, that thou shouldest be afraid of a man that shall die, and of the son of man which shall be made as grass? (Isa. 51:12).

For all flesh is as grass and all the glory of man as the flower of grass. The grass withereth, and the flower thereof falleth away (I Peter 1:24).

GOD'S PROMISE FOR TODAY

As for man, his days are as grass: as a flower of the field, so he flourisheth. For the wind passeth over it, and it is gone; and the place thereof shall know it no more (Ps. 103:15, 16).

"It often shows a fine command of language to say nothing."

JULY 19

Neither can they die any more: for they are equal unto the angels, and are the children of God, being the children of the resurrection (Luke 20:36).

Verily, verily, I say unto you, if a man keep My saying, he shall never see death (John 8:51).

And whosoever liveth and believeth in Me shall never die. Believest thou this? (John 11:26).

To them who by patient continuance in well doing seek for glory and honour and immortality, eternal life (Rom. 2:7).

Then we which are alive and remain shall be caught up together with them in the clouds, to meet the Lord in the air: and so shall we ever be with the Lord (I Thess. 4:17).

GOD'S PROMISE FOR TODAY

For we know that, if our earthly house of this tabernacle were dissolved, we have a building of God, a house not made with hands, eternal in the heavens (II Cor. 5:1).

"A man without principle should not draw much interest."

JULY 20

But God will redeem my soul from the power of the grave: for He shall receive me (Ps. 49:15).

Verily, verily, I say unto you, the hour is coming, and now is, when the dead shall hear the voice of the Son of God: and they that hear shall live (John 5:25).

And this is the will of Him that sent Me, that every one which seeth the Son, and believeth on Him, may have everlasting life: and I will raise him up at the last day (John 6:40).

Jesus said unto her, I am the resurrection, and the life: he that believeth in me, though he were dead, yet shall he live (John 11:25).

Knowing that He which raised up the Lord Jesus shall raise up us also by Jesus and shall present us with you (II Cor. 4:14).

GOD'S PROMISE FOR TODAY

For the Lord Himself shall descend from heaven with a shout, with the voice of the archangel, and with the trump of God: and the dead in Christ shall rise first (I Thess. 4:16).

"Be an 'Amen' Christian, but don't shout it louder than you live it."

JULY 21

Who was delivered for our offences, and was raised again for our justification (Rom. 4:25).

And that He was buried, and that He rose again the third day according to the Scriptures (I Cor. 15:4).

Which He wrought in Christ, when He raised Him from the dead, and set Him at His own right hand in the heavenly places (Eph. 1:20).

For if we believe that Jesus died and rose again, even so them also which sleep in Jesus will God bring with Him (I Thess. 4:14).

Blessed be the God and Father of our Lord Jesus Christ, which according to His abundant mercy hath begotten us again unto a lively hope by the resurrection of Jesus Christ from the dead (I Peter 1:3).

GOD'S PROMISE FOR TODAY

That if thou shalt confess with thy mouth the Lord Jesus, and shalt believe in thine heart that God hath raised Him from the dead, thou shalt be saved (Rom. 10:9).

"If Christ is the way, why waste time traveling some other way?"

JULY 22

Sing aloud unto God our strength: make a joyful noise unto the God of Jacob (Ps. 81:1).

O come, let us sing unto the Lord: let us make a joyful noise to the Rock of our salvation (Ps. 95:1).

Ye shall have a song, as in the night when a holy solemnity is kept; and gladness of heart, as when one goeth with a pipe to come into the mountain of the Lord, to the Mighty One of Israel (Isa. 30:29).

What is it then? I will pray with the spirit, and I will pray with the understanding also: I will sing with the spirit, and I will sing with the understanding also (I Cor. 14:15).

Is any among you afflicted? let him pray. Is any merry? let him sing psalms (James 5:13).

GOD'S PROMISE FOR TODAY

Speaking to yourselves in psalms and hymns and spiritual songs, singing and making melody in your heart to the Lord (Eph. 5:19).

"They always talk who never think."

JULY 23

Of old hast Thou laid the foundation of the earth: and the heavens are the work of Thy hands. They shall perish but Thou shalt endure: yea, all of them shall wax old like a garment; as a vesture shalt Thou change them, and they shall be changed (Ps. 102:25, 26).

And all the host of heaven shall be dissolved, and the heavens shall be rolled together as a scroll: and all their host shall fall down, as the leaf falleth off from the vine, and as a falling fig from the fig tree (Isa. 34:4).

And they that use this world, as not abusing it: for the fashion of this world passeth away (I Cor. 7:31).

GOD'S PROMISE FOR TODAY

But the day of the Lord will come as a thief in the night; in the which the heavens shall pass away with a great noise, and the elements shall melt with fervent heat, the earth also and the works that are therein shall be burned up (II Peter 3:10).

"Life is like a band—we need not all play the same part, but we must play in harmony."

JULY 24

For I lift up My hand to heaven, and say, I live forever (Deut. 32:40).

The eternal God is thy refuge, and underneath are the ever-lasting arms (Deut. 33:27).

Thy name, O Lord, endureth for ever; and Thy memorial, O Lord, throughout all generations (Ps. 135:13).

Thy kingdom is an everlasting kingdom and thy dominion endureth throughout all generations (Ps. 145:13).

But, beloved, be not ignorant of this one thing, that one day is with the Lord as a thousand years, and a thousand years as one day (II Peter 3:8).

We know, that we have passed from death unto life, because we love the brethren. He that loveth not his brother abideth in death (I John 3:14).

GOD'S PROMISE FOR TODAY

I am Alpha and Omega, the beginning and the ending, saith the Lord, which is, and which was, and which is to come, the Almighty (Rev. 1:8).

"Experience gained the hard way brings knowledge that remains with us."

JULY 25

And in the days of these kings shall the God of heaven set up a kingdom, which shall never be destroyed: and the kingdom shall not be left to other people, but it shall break in pieces and consume all these kingdoms, and it shall stand for ever (Dan. 2:44).

I saw in the night visions, and, behold, one like the Son of man came with the clouds of heaven, and came to the Ancient of days, and they brought him near before him. And there was given him dominion, and glory, and a kingdom, that all people, nations, and languages should serve him: his dominion is an everlasting dominion, which shall not pass away, and his kingdom that which shall not be destroyed (Dan. 7:13, 14).

GOD'S PROMISE FOR TODAY

Of the increase of his government and peace there shall be no end, upon the throne of David, and upon his kingdom, to order it, and to establish it with judgment and with justice from henceforth even for ever. The zeal of the Lord of hosts will perform this (Isa. 9:7).

"A grateful mind is a great mind."

Boast not thyself of tomorrow; for thou knowest not what a day may bring forth (Prov. 27:1).

Wherefore I perceive that there is nothing better than that a man should rejoice in his own works; for that is his portion: for who shall bring him to see what shall be after him? (Eccles. 3:22).

For man also knoweth not his time: as the fishes that are taken in an evil net, and as the birds are caught in the snare; so are the sons of men snared in an evil time, when it falleth suddenly upon them (Eccles. 9:12).

But know this, that if the goodman of the house had known in what watch the thief would come, he would have watched, and would not have suffered his house to be broken up (Matt. 24:43).

GOD'S PROMISE FOR TODAY

Whereas ye know not what shall be on the morrow. For what is your life? It is even a vapour, that appeareth for a little time, and then vanisheth away (James 4:14).

"Hem your blessings with praise lest they unravel."

It is the glory of God to conceal a thing: but the honour of kings is to search out a matter (Prov. 25:2).

And he said, Go thy way, Daniel: for the words are closed up and sealed till the time of the end (Dan. 12:9).

But of that day and that hour knoweth no man, no, not the angels which are in heaven, neither the Son, but the Father (Mark 13:32).

And no man in heaven, nor in earth, neither under the earth, was able to open the book, neither to look thereon (Rev. 5:3).

And when the seven thunders had uttered their voices, I was about to write: and I heard a voice from heaven saying unto me, Seal up those things which the seven thunders uttered, and write them not (Rev. 10:4).

GOD'S PROMISE FOR TODAY

The secret things belong unto the Lord our God: but those things which are revealed belong unto us and to our children for ever, that we may do all the words of this law (Deut. 29:29).

"Be the first to praise and the first to deserve praise."

And that repentance and remission of sins should be preached in His name among all nations, beginning in Jerusalem (Luke 24:47).

And whatsoever ye shall ask in My name, that will I do, that the Father may be glorified in the Son (John 14:13).

Then Peter said, Silver and gold have I none; but such as I have give I thee: in the name of Jesus Christ of Nazareth rise up and walk (Acts 3:6).

And His name, through faith in His name, hath made this man strong whom ye see and know: yea, the faith which is by Him hath given him this perfect soundness in the presence of you all (Acts 3:16).

Giving thanks always for all things unto God and the Father in the name of our Lord Jesus Christ (Eph. 5:20).

GOD'S PROMISE FOR TODAY

But these are written, that ye might believe that Jesus is the Christ, the Son of God; and that believing ye might have life through His name (John 20:31).

"Be generous with kind words, especially about those who are absent."

Notwithstanding, lest we should offend them, go thou to the sea, and cast a hook, and take up the fish that first cometh up; and when thou hast opened his mouth, thou shalt find a piece of money; that take, and give unto them for Me and thee (Matt. 17:27).

Let every soul be subject unto the higher powers. For there is no power but of God: the powers that be are ordained of God (Rom. 13:1).

Put them in mind to be subject to principalities and powers, to obey magistrates, to be ready to every good work (Titus 3:1).

Submit yourselves to every ordinance of man for the Lord's sake: whether it be to the king, as supreme; or unto governors, as unto them that are sent by him for the punishment of evil doers, and for the praise of them that do well (I Peter 2:13, 14).

GOD'S PROMISE FOR TODAY

Then saith He unto them, Render therefore unto Caesar the

things which are Caesar's; and unto God the things that are God's (Matt. 22:21).

"Life is like a ladder: every step we take is either up or down."

JULY 30

Create in me a clean heart, O God; and renew a right spirit within me (Ps. 51:10).

But they that wait upon the Lord shall renew their strength; they shall mount up with wings as eagles; they shall run, and not be weary; and they shall walk, and not faint (Isa. 40:31).

For which cause we faint not; but though our outward man perish, yet the inward man is renewed day by day (II Cor. 4:16).

And have put on the new man, which is renewed in knowledge after the image of Him that created Him (Col. 3:10).

Not by works of righteousness which we have done, but according to His mercy He saved us, by the washing of regeneration, and renewing of the Holy Ghost (Titus 3:5).

GOD'S PROMISE FOR TODAY

And be not conformed to this world: but be ye transformed by the renewing of your mind, that ye may prove what is that good, and acceptable, and perfect will of God (Romans 12:2).

"Nothing can make a *trusting* Christian blue."

JULY 31

Sing unto Him a new song; play skilfully with a loud noise (Ps. 33:3).

I will sing a new song unto Thee, O God: upon a psaltery and an instrument of ten strings will I sing praises unto Thee (Ps. 144:9).

Praise ye the Lord. Sing unto the Lord a new song and His praise in the congregation of saints (Ps. 149:1).

And they sung as it were a new song before the throne, and before the four beasts, and the elders: and no man could learn that song but the hundred and forty and four thousand, which were redeemed from the earth (Rev. 14:3).

And they sing the song of Moses the servant of God, and the song of the Lamb, saying, Great and marvellous are Thy works, Lord God Almighty; just and true are Thy ways, thou King of saints (Rev. 15:3).

GOD'S PROMISE FOR TODAY

And He hath put a new song in my mouth, even praise unto our God: many shall see it, and fear, and shall trust in the Lord (Ps. 40:3).

"A Christian should be a lamp, not a damp."

August

AUGUST 1

Better is the end of a thing than the beginning thereof: and the patient in spirit is better than the proud in spirit (Eccles. 7:8).

In your patience possess ye your souls (Luke 21:19).

That the aged men be sober, grave, temperate, sound in faith, in love, in patience (Titus 2:2).

For ye have need of patience, that, after ye have done the will of God, ye might receive the promise (Heb. 10:36).

But let patience have her perfect work, that ye may be perfect and entire, wanting nothing (James 1:4).

Be patient therefore, brethren, unto the coming of the Lord. Behold, the husbandman waiteth for the precious fruit of the earth, and hath long patience for it, until he receive the early and latter rain (James 5:7).

GOD'S PROMISE FOR TODAY

Rejoicing in hope; patient in tribulation; continuing instant in prayer (Rom. 12:12).

"He who delays his repentance pawns his soul with the devil."

AUGUST 2

The Lord is nigh unto them that are of a broken heart; and saveth such as be of a contrite spirit (Ps. 34:18).

The sacrifices of God are a broken spirit: a broken and a contrite heart, O God, Thou wilt not despise (Ps. 51:17).

For all those things hath Mine hand made, and all those things have been, saith the Lord: but to this man will I look, even to him that is poor and of a contrite spirit, and trembleth at My word (Isa. 66:2).

And rend your heart, and not your garments, and turn unto the Lord your God: for He is gracious and merciful, slow to anger, and of great kindness, and repenteth Him of the evil (Joel 2:13).

When I fall, I shall arise; when I sit in darkness, the Lord shall be a light unto me (Mic. 7:8).

GOD'S PROMISE FOR TODAY

For godly sorrow worketh repentance to salvation not to be repented of; but the sorrow of the world worketh death (II Cor. 7:10).

"He who is born of God is certain to resemble his Father."

AUGUST 3

Harden not your heart, as in the provocation, and as in the day of temptation in the wilderness (Ps. 95:8).

Happy is the man that feareth always: but he that hardeneth his heart shall fall into mischief (Prov. 28:14).

But, after thy hardness and impenitent heart, treasurest up unto thyself wrath against the day of wrath and revelation of the righteous judgment of God (Rom. 2:5).

But exhort one another daily, while it is called Today; lest any of you be hardened through the deceitfulness of sin (Heb. 3:13).

And base things of the world, and things which are despised, hath God chosen, yea, and things which are not, to bring to nought things that are (I Cor. 1:28).

GOD'S PROMISE FOR TODAY

He, that being often reproved hardeneth his neck, shall suddenly be destroyed, and that without remedy (Prov. 29:1).

"People look at you six days in the week to see what you mean on the seventh day."

AUGUST 4

And when Abram was ninety years old and nine, the Lord appeared to Abram, and said unto him, I am the Almighty God; walk before Me, and be thou perfect (Gen. 17:1).

Finally, brethren, farewell. Be perfect, be of good comfort, be of one mind, live in peace; and the God of love and peace shall be with you (II Cor. 13:11).

Till we all come in the unity of the faith, and of the knowledge of the Son of God, unto a perfect man, unto the measure of the stature of the fulness of Christ (Eph. 4:13).

Whom we preach, warning every man, and teaching every man in all wisdom; that we may present every man perfect in Christ Jesus (Col. 1:28).

But let patience have her perfect work, that ye may be perfect and entire, wanting nothing (James 1:4).

GOD'S PROMISE FOR TODAY

Therefore leaving the principles of the doctrine of Christ, let us go on unto perfection; not laying again the foundation of repentance from dead works, and of faith toward God (Heb. 6:1).

"A crossless life means a crownless death."

AUGUST 5

Yet a little sleep, a little slumber, a little folding of the hands to sleep: so shall thy poverty come as a robber, and thy want as an armed man (Prov. 6:10, 11).

There is that scattereth, and yet increaseth; and there is that withholdeth more than is meet, but it tendeth to poverty (Prov. 11:24).

He that loveth pleasure shall be a poor man: he that loveth wine and oil shall not be rich (Prov. 21:17).

For the drunkard and the glutton shall come to poverty: and drowsiness shall clothe a man with rags (Prov. 23:21).

And if thou draw out thy soul to the hungry, and satisfy the afflicted soul; then shall thy light rise in obscurity, and thy darkness be as the noonday (Isa. 58:10).

GOD'S PROMISE FOR TODAY

He that tilleth his land shall have plenty of bread: but he that followeth after vain persons shall have poverty enough (Prov. 28:19).

"You can't take money with you to heaven, but you can send it up ahead."

AUGUST 6

And when thy herds and thy flocks multiply, and thy silver

and thy gold is multiplied, and all that thou hast is multiplied; then thine heart be lifted up, and thou forget the Lord thy God (Deut. 8:13, 14).

A faithful man shall abound with blessings; but he that maketh haste to be rich shall not be innocent (Prov. 28:20).

Then said Jesus unto His disciples, Verily I say unto you, that a rich man shall hardly enter into the kingdom of heaven (Matt. 19:23).

And the cares of this world, and the deceitfulness of riches, and the lusts of other things entering in, choke the word, and it becometh unfruitful (Mark 4:19).

But they that will be rich fall into temptation and a snare, and into many foolish and hurtful lusts, which drown men in destruction and perdition (I Tim. 6:9).

GOD'S PROMISE FOR TODAY

Trust not in oppression, and become not vain in robbery: if riches increase, set not your heart upon them (Ps. 62:10).

"Where love resides God abides."

AUGUST 7

The increase of his house shall depart, and his goods shall flow away in the day of his wrath (Job 20:28).

For he seeth that wise men die, likewise the fool and the brutish person perish, and leave their wealth to others (Ps. 49:10).

Wilt thou set thine eyes upon that which is not? for riches certainly make themselves wings; they fly away as an eagle toward heaven (Prov. 23:5).

For riches are not for ever: and doth the crown endure to every generation? (Prov. 27:24).

Yea, I hated all my labour which I had taken under the sun: because I should leave it unto the man that shall be after me (Eccles. 2:18).

As the partridge sitteth on eggs, and hatcheth them not; so he that getteth riches, and not by right, shall leave them in the midst of his days, and at his end shall be a fool (Jer. 17:11).

GOD'S PROMISE FOR TODAY

For we brought nothing into this world, and it is certain we can carry nothing out (I Tim. 6:7).

"It is not what happens to us that matters, but how we react to it."

AUGUST 8

Though he heap up silver as the dust, and prepare raiment as the clay; he may prepare it, but the just shall put it on, and the innocent shall divide the silver (Job. 27:16, 17).

For God giveth to a man that is good in His sight, wisdom, and knowledge, and joy; but to the sinner He giveth travail, to gather and to heap up, that He may give to him that is good before God (Eccles. 2:26).

With thy wisdom and with thine understanding thou hast gotten thee riches, and hast gotten gold and silver into thy treasures (Ezek. 28:4).

Your gold and silver is cankered; and the rust of them shall be a witness against you, and shall eat your flesh as it were fire. Ye have heaped treasure together for the last days (James 5:3).

GOD'S PROMISE FOR TODAY

Lay not up for yourselves treasures upon earth, where moth and rust doth corrupt, and where thieves break through and steal (Matt. 6:19).

"Persecution will bring out virtue or villainy."

AUGUST 9

Riches and honour are with Me; yea, durable riches and righteousness (Prov. 8:18).

The eyes of your understanding being enlightened; that ye may know what is the hope of His calling, and what the riches of the glory of His inheritance in the saints (Eph. 1:18).

Unto me, who am less than the least of all saints, is this grace given that I should preach among the Gentiles, the unsearchable riches of Christ (Eph. 3:8).

Esteeming the reproach of Christ greater riches than the treasures in Egypt; for he had respect unto the recompence of the reward (Heb. 11:26).

Hearken, my beloved brethren, hath not God chosen the poor of this world rich in faith, and heirs of the kingdom which He hath promised to them that love Him? (James 2:5).

GOD'S PROMISE FOR TODAY

The blessing of the Lord, it maketh rich, and He addeth no sorrow to it (Prov. 10:22).

"A river becomes crooked by following the line of least resistance—so does man."

Jesus said unto him, If thou wilt be perfect, go and sell that thou hast and give to the poor, and thou shalt have treasure in heaven: and come and follow Me (Matt. 19:21).

Sell that ye have, and give alms; provide yourselves bags which wax not old, a treasure in the heavens that faileth not (Luke 12:33).

Yea verily, and I count all things to be loss for the excellency of the knowledge of Christ Jesus my Lord, for Whom I suffered the loss of all things and do count them but refuse that I may gain Christ (Phil. 3:8, RV).

I counsel thee to buy of Me gold tried in the fire, that thou mayest be rich; and white raiment, that thou mayest be clothed, and that the shame of thy nakedness do not appear; and anoint thine eyes with eyesalve, that thou mayest see (Rev. 3:18).

GOD'S PROMISE FOR TODAY

But lay up for yourselves treasures in heaven where neither moth nor rust doth corrupt, and where thieves do not break through nor steal (Matt. 6:20).

"He stands best who kneels most."

Seek the Lord and His strength, seek His face continually (I Chron. 16:11).

Watch and pray, that ye enter not into temptation: the spirit indeed is willing, but the flesh is weak (Matt. 26:41).

And He spake a parable unto them to this end, that men ought always to pray and not to faint (Luke 18:1).

Hitherto have ye asked nothing in My name: ask, and ye shall receive, that your joy may be full (John 16:24).

Praying always with all prayer and supplication in the Spirit, and watching thereunto with all perseverance and supplication for all saints (Eph. 6:18).

Pray without ceasing (I Thess. 5:17).

Is any among you afflicted? let him pray. Is any merry? let him sing psalms (James 5:13).

GOD'S PROMISE FOR TODAY

Ask, and it shall be given you: seek, and ye shall find; knock, and it shall be opened unto you (Matt. 7:7).

"Many people are on the salvation train; but a lot of them are traveling in the sleeper."

He shall call upon me, and I will answer him: I will be with him in trouble; I will deliver him, and honour him (Ps. 91:15).

Then shalt thou call, and the Lord shall answer; thou shalt cry, and He shall say, Here I am. If thou take away from the midst of thee the yoke, and putting forth of the finger, and speaking vanity (Isa. 58:9).

And I will bring the third part through the fire, and will refine them as silver is refined, and will try them as gold is tried: they shall call on My name, and I will hear them: I will say, It is My people: and they shall say, The Lord is my God (Zech. 13:9).

And I say unto you, Ask, and it shall be given you; seek, and ye shall find; knock, and it shall be opened unto you (Luke 11:9).

GOD'S PROMISE FOR TODAY

If ye abide in Me, and My words abide in you, ye shall ask what ye will, and it shall be done unto you (John 15:7).

"Yesterday's unfinished task is a mortgage on today."

These all continued with one accord in prayer and supplication, with the women, and Mary the mother of Jesus, and with His brethren (Acts 1:14).

And when they heard that, they lifted up their voice to God with one accord, and said, Lord, Thou art God, which hast made heaven, and earth, and the sea, and all that in them is (Acts 4:24).

And when he had considered the thing, he came to the house of Mary the mother of John, whose surname was Mark; where many were gathered together praying (Acts 12:12).

And when we had accomplished those days, we departed and went our way; and they all brought us on our way, with wives and children, till we were out of the city; and we kneeled down on the shore, and prayed (Acts 21:5).

GOD'S PROMISE FOR TODAY

Again I say unto you, That if two of you shall agree on earth as touching any thing that they shall ask, it shall be done for them of My Father which is in heaven (Matt. 18:19).

"A good place to find a helping hand is at the end of your arm."

AUGUST 14

If My people, which are called by My name, shall humble themselves, and pray, and seek My face, and turn from their wicked ways; then will I hear from heaven, and will forgive their sin, and will heal their land (II Chron. 7:14).

And ye shall seek Me, and find Me, when ye shall search for Me with all your heart (Jer. 29:13).

Therefore I say unto you, What things soever ye desire, when ye pray, believe that ye receive them, and ye shall have them (Mark 11:24).

Confess your faults one to another, and pray one for another, that ye may be healed. The effectual fervent prayer of a righteous man availeth much (James 5:16).

Unto Thee lift I up mine eyes, O Thou that dwellest in the heavens (Ps. 123:1).

GOD'S PROMISE FOR TODAY

And whatsoever we ask, we receive of Him, because we keep His commandments, and do those things that are pleasing in His sight (I John 3:22).

"God is as great in minuteness as He is in magnitude."

AUGUST 15

And when He had sent them away, He departed into a mountain to pray. And when even was come, the ship was in the midst of the sea, and He alone on the land (Mark 6:46, 47).

. . . and great multitudes came together to hear and to be healed by Him of their infirmities. And He withdrew Himself into the wilderness, and prayed (Luke 5:15, 16).

And it came to pass, as He was alone praying, His disciples were with Him; and He asked them, saying, Whom say the people that I am? (Luke 9:18).

And He was withdrawn from them about a stone's cast, and kneeled down, and prayed, saying, Father, if Thou be willing, remove this cup from Me: nevertheless, not My will, but Thine, be done (Luke 22:41, 42).

GOD'S PROMISE FOR TODAY

And in the morning, rising up a great while before day, He went out, and departed into a solitary place, and there prayed (Mark 1:35).

"The measure of your usefulness is determined by the measure of your consecration."

AUGUST 16

So also Christ glorified not Himself to be made a high priest; but He that said unto Him, Thou art My Son, today have I begotten Thee (Heb. 5:5).

Whither the forerunner is for us entered, even Jesus, made a high priest for ever after the order of Melchisedec (Heb. 6:20).

For such a high priest became us, Who is holy, harmless, undefiled, separate from sinners, and made higher than the heavens (Heb. 7:26).

Now of the things which we have spoken this is the sum: We have such a high priest, Who is set on the right hand of the throne of the Majesty in the heavens (Heb. 8:1).

GOD'S PROMISE FOR TODAY

Seeing then that we have a great high priest, that is passed into the heavens, Jesus the Son of God, let us hold fast our profession. For we have not a high priest which cannot be touched with the feeling of our infirmities; but was in all points tempted like as we are, yet without sin (Heb. 4:14, 15).

"Have the grace to say, 'I was wrong and you were right.' "

AUGUST 17

And ye shall be unto Me a kingdom of priests, and a holy nation. These are the words which thou shalt speak unto the children of Israel (Exod. 19:6).

But ye shall be named the Priests of the Lord: men shall call you the Ministers of our God: ye shall eat the riches of the Gentiles, and in their glory shall ye boast yourselves (Isa. 61:6).

Ye also, as lively stones, are built up a spiritual house, a holy priesthood, to offer up spiritual sacrifices, acceptable to God by Jesus Christ (I Peter 2:5).

And hath made us kings and priests unto God and His Father; to Him be glory and dominion for ever and ever. Amen (Rev. 1:6).

GOD'S PROMISE FOR TODAY

Blessed and holy is he that hath part in the first resurrection: on such the second death hath no power, but they shall be priests of God and of Christ, and shall reign with Him a thousand years (Rev. 20:6).

"Effective speaking *for* God depends upon right hearkening *to* God."

AUGUST 18

Thou shalt keep therefore His statutes, and His commandments, which I command thee this day, that it may go well with thee, and with thy children after thee, and that thou mayest prolong thy days upon the earth, which the Lord thy God giveth thee, for ever (Deut. 4:40).

Say ye to the righteous, that it shall be well with him: for they shall eat the fruit of their doings (Isa. 3:10).

For bodily exercise profiteth little: but godliness is profitable unto all things, having promise of the life that now is, and of that which is to come (I Tim. 4:8).

This is a faithful saying, and these things I will that thou affirm constantly, that they which have believed in God might be careful to maintain good works. These things are good and profitable unto men (Titus 3:8).

GOD'S PROMISE FOR TODAY

But godliness with contentment is great gain (I Tim. 6:6).

"Prayer is an acknowledgment of faith; worry a denial of faith."

AUGUST 19

And turn ye not aside: for then should ye go after vain things, which cannot profit nor deliver; for they are vain (I Sam. 12:21).

Treasures of wickedness profit nothing: but righteousness delivereth from death (Prov. 10:2).

For there shall be no reward to the evil man; the candle of the wicked shall be put out (Prov. 24:20).

They that make a graven image are all of them vanity; and their delectable things shall not profit; and they are their own witnesses; they see not, nor know; that they may be ashamed (Isa. 44:9).

They have sown wheat, but shall reap thorns: they have put themselves to pain, but shall not profit: and they shall be ashamed of your revenues because of the fierce anger of the Lord (Jer. 12:13).

GOD'S PROMISE FOR TODAY

For what is a man profited, if he gain the whole world, and lose or forfeit his own self (Luke 9:25, RV).

"The blood makes me safe; the Word makes me sure; obedience makes me happy."

Many are the afflictions of the righteous: but the Lord delivereth him out of them all. He keepeth all his bones: not one of them is broken (Ps. 34:19, 20).

The Lord will strengthen him upon the bed of languishing: Thou wilt make all his bed in his sickness (Ps. 41:3).

When thou passest through the waters, I will be with thee; and through the rivers, they shall not overflow thee: when thou walkest through the fire, thou shalt not be burned; neither shall the flame kindle upon thee (Isa. 43:2).

Let not your heart be troubled: ye believe in God, believe also in Me. In My Father's house are many mansions; if it were not so, I would have told you. I go to prepare a place for you (John 14:1, 2).

GOD'S PROMISE FOR TODAY

For His anger endureth but a moment; in His favour is life: weeping may endure for a night, but joy cometh in the morning (Ps. 30:5).

"Humility is a strange thing. The moment you think you have it, you've lost it."

And we know that all things work together for good to them that love God, to them who are the called according to His purpose (Rom. 8:28).

Beloved, think it not strange concerning the fiery trial which is to try you, as though some strange thing happened unto you: but rejoice, inasmuch as ye are partakers of Christ's sufferings (I Peter 4:12, 13).

And God shall wipe away all tears from their eyes; and there shall be no more death, neither sorrow, nor crying, neither shall there be any more pain: for the former things are passed away (Rev. 21:4).

GOD'S PROMISE FOR TODAY

And He said unto me, My grace is sufficient for thee: for My strength is made perfect in weakness. Most gladly therefore will I rather glory in my infirmities, that the power of Christ may rest upon me (II Cor. 12:9).

"You can't cash any checks on heaven's bank without having made a deposit there."

Trust in the Lord, and do good; so shalt thou dwell in the land, and verily thou shalt be fed (Ps. 37:3).

Jesus said unto him. If thou canst believe, all things are possible to him that believeth (Mark 9:23).

Therefore I say unto you, What things soever ye desire, when ye pray, believe that ye receive them, and ye shall have them (Mark 11:24).

And the Lord said, If ye had faith as a grain of mustard seed, ye might say unto this sycamine tree, be thou plucked up by the root, and be thou planted in the sea; and it should obey you (Luke 17:6).

While we look not at the things which are seen, but at the things which are not seen: for the things which are seen are temporal; but the things which are not seen are eternal (II Cor. 4:18).

GOD'S PROMISE FOR TODAY

But as many as received Him, to them gave He power to become the sons of God, even to them that believe on His name (John 1:12).

"It takes only a look to be saved, but it takes meditation to be sanctified."

And as Moses lifted up the serpent in the wilderness, even so must the son of man be lifted up: that whosoever believeth in Him should not perish, but have eternal life (John 3:14, 15).

And Jesus said unto them, I am the bread of life: he that cometh to Me shall never hunger; and he that believeth on Me shall never thirst (John 6:35).

I am come a light into the world, that whosoever believeth on Me should not abide in darkness (John 12:46).

Verily, Verily, I say unto you, He that believeth on Me, the works that I do shall he do also; and greater works than these shall he do; because I go unto My Father (John 14:12).

GOD'S PROMISE FOR TODAY

For I am not ashamed of the gospel of Christ: for it is the power of God unto salvation to every one that believeth; to the Jew first, and also to the Greek (Rom. 1:16).

"All people smile in the same language."

Though the Lord be high, yet hath He respect unto the lowly: but the proud He knoweth afar off (Ps. 138:6).

For all those things hath Mine hand made, and all those things have been, saith the Lord: but to this man will I look, even to him that is poor and of a contrite spirit, and trembleth at My word (Isa. 66:2).

But He giveth more grace. Wherefore He saith, God resisteth the proud, but giveth grace unto the humble (James 4:6).

Likewise, ye younger, submit yourselves unto the elder. Yea, all of you be subject one to another, and be clothed with humility: for God resisteth the proud, and giveth grace to the humble (I Peter 5:5).

Follow after charity, and desire spiritual gifts, but rather that ye may prophesy (I Cor. 14:1).

GOD'S PROMISE FOR TODAY

For whosoever exalteth himself shall be abased; and he that humbleth himself shall be exalted (Luke 14:11).

"Cheerfulness will open a door when other keys fail."

Blessed is he that considereth the poor: the Lord will deliver him in time of trouble (Ps. 41:1).

Honour the Lord with thy substance, and with the firstfruits of all thine increase: so shall thy barns be filled with plenty, and thy presses shall burst out with new wine (Prov. 3:9, 10).

And if thou draw out thy soul to the hungry, and satisfy the afflicted soul; then shall thy light rise in obscurity. And thy darkness be as the noonday (Isa. 58:10).

Give and it shall be given unto you; good measure, pressed down, and shaken together, and running over, shall men give into your bosom. For with the same measure that ye mete withal it shall be measured to you again (Luke 6:38).

Every man according as he purposeth in his heart, so let him give, not grudgingly or of necessity: for God loveth a cheerful giver (II Cor. 9:7).

GOD'S PROMISE FOR TODAY

The liberal soul shall be made fat: and he that watereth shall be watered also himself (Prov. 11:25).

"Human beings, like chickens, thrive best when they scratch for what they get."

Return, ye backsliding children, and I will heal your backslidings. Behold, we come unto Thee; for Thou art the Lord our God (Jer. 3:22).

And rend your heart, and not your garments, and turn unto the Lord your God: for He is gracious and merciful, slow to anger, and of great kindness, and repenteth Him of the evil (Joel 2:13).

Who is a God like unto Thee, that pardoneth iniquity and passeth by the transgression of the remnant of His heritage? He retaineth not His anger for ever, because He delighteth in mercy (Mic. 7:18).

I say unto you, that likewise joy shall be in heaven over one sinner that repenteth, more than over ninety and nine just persons, which need no repentance (Luke 15:7).

GOD'S PROMISE FOR TODAY

The Lord is nigh unto them that are of a broken heart: and saveth such as be of a contrite spirit (Ps. 34:18).

"The poorest man is he who has nothing but money."

And the Lord said, Simon, Simon, behold, Satan hath desired to have you, that he may sift you as wheat. But I have prayed for thee, that thy faith fail not: and when thou art converted, strengthen thy brethren (Luke 22:31, 32).

And the God of peace shall bruise Satan under your feet shortly (Rom. 16:20).

For in that He Himself hath suffered being tempted, He is able to succour them that are tempted (Heb. 2:18).

Submit yourselves therefore to God. Resist the devil, and he will flee from you (James 4:7).

GOD'S PROMISE FOR TODAY

There hath no temptation taken you but such as is common to man: but God is faithful, Who will not suffer you to be tempted above that ye are able; but will with the temptation also make a way of escape, that ye may be able to bear it (I Cor. 10:13).

"Learning is an ornament in prosperity, a refuge in adversity, and a provision in old age."

And they that be wise shall shine as the brightness of the firmament; and they that turn many to righteousness, as the stars for ever and ever (Dan. 12:3).

For whosoever shall give you a cup of water to drink in My name, because ye belong to Christ, verily I say unto you, he shall not lose his reward (Mark 9:41).

But glory, honour, and peace, to every man that worketh good; to the Jew first, and also the Gentile (Rom. 2:10).

If any man's work abide which he hath built thereupon, he shall receive a reward (I Cor. 3:14).

Therefore, my beloved brethren, be ye stedfast, unmoveable, always abounding in the work of the Lord, forasmuch as ye know that your labour is not in vain in the Lord (I Cor. 15:58).

GOD'S PROMISE FOR TODAY

But whoso looketh into the perfect law of liberty, and continueth therein, he being not a forgetful hearer, but a doer of the work, this man shall be blessed in his deed (James 1:25).

"Be bold in what you stand for but careful in what you fall for."

AUGUST 29

And it shall come to pass, while My glory passeth by, that I will put thee in a cleft of the rock, and will cover thee with My hand while I pass by (Exod. 33:22).

And I have put My words in thy mouth, and I have covered thee in the shadow of Mine hand, that I may plant the heavens, and lay the foundations of the earth, and say unto Zion, Thou art My people (Isa. 51:16).

O Jerusalem, Jerusalem, thou that killest the prophets, and stonest them which are sent unto thee, how often would I have gathered thy children together, even as a hen gathereth her chickens under her wings, and ye would not (Matt. 23:37).

GOD'S PROMISE FOR TODAY

For Thou hast been a strength to the poor, a strength to the needy in his distress, a refuge from the storm, a shadow from the heat, when the blast of the terrible ones is as a storm against the wall (Isa. 25:4).

"He who carries a tale makes a monkey of himself."

And, behold, I am with thee, and will keep thee in all places whither thou goest, and will bring thee again into this land; for I will not leave thee, until I have done that which I have spoken to thee of (Gen. 28:15).

Behold, He that keepeth Israel shall neither slumber nor sleep (Ps. 121:4).

And now I am no more in the world, but these are in the world, and I come to Thee. Holy Father, keep through Thine own name those whom Thou hast given Me, that they may be one, as We are (John 17:11).

This is that bread which came down from heaven: not as your fathers did eat manna, and are dead: he that eateth of this bread shall live for ever (John 6:58).

GOD'S PROMISE FOR TODAY

I know Him Whom I have believed, and I am persuaded that He is able to guard my deposit which I have committed unto Him against that day (II Tim. 1:12, RV).

"Trouble is like an ugly dog—looks worse coming than going."

Ye have seen what I did unto the Egyptians, and how I bare you on eagles' wings, and brought you unto Myself (Exod. 19:4).

The eternal God is thy refuge, and underneath are the everlasting arms: and He shall thrust out the enemy from before thee; and shall say, Destroy them (Deut. 33:27).

Thou hast also given me the shield of Thy salvation; and Thy right hand hath holden me up, and Thy gentleness hath made me great (Ps. 18:35).

They shall bear thee up in their hands, lest thou dash thy foot against a stone (Ps. 91:12).

And even to your old age I am He; and even to hoar hairs will I carry you: I have made, and I will bear; even I will carry, and will deliver you (Isa. 46:4).

GOD'S PROMISE FOR TODAY

Fear thou not; for I am with thee; be not dismayed; for I am thy God: I will strengthen thee; yea, I will help thee, Yea, I will uphold thee with the right hand of My righteousness (Isa. 41:10).

"God appears in the life when self disappears."

September

SEPTEMBER 1

And the Lord commanded us to do all these statutes, to fear the Lord our God, for our good always, that He might preserve us alive, as it is at this day (Deut. 6:24).

O love the Lord, all ye His saints: for the Lord preserveth the faithful and plentifully rewardeth the proud doer (Ps. 31:23).

For the Lord loveth judgment, and forsaketh not His saints; they are preserved for ever: but the seed of the wicked shall be cut off (Ps. 37:28).

And the Lord shall deliver me from every evil work, and will preserve me unto His heavenly kingdom: to Whom be glory for ever and ever. Amen (II Tim. 4:18).

And it shall come to pass, that before they call, I will answer; and while they are yet speaking, I will hear (Isa. 65:24).

GOD'S PROMISE FOR TODAY

He keepeth the paths of judgment, and preserveth the way of His saints (Prov. 2:8).

"A beautiful heart seems to transform the homely face."

SEPTEMBER 2

A prudent man concealeth knowledge: but the heart of fools proclaimeth foolishness (Prov. 12:23).

A fool despiseth his father's instruction: but he that regardeth reproof is prudent (Prov. 15:5).

The heart of the prudent getteth knowledge; and the ear of the wise seeketh knowledge (Prov. 18:15).

A fool also is full of words: a man cannot tell what shall be; and what shall be after him, who can tell him? (Eccles. 10:14).

A prudent man forseeth the evil, and hideth himself: but the simple pass on, and are punished (Prov. 22:3).

Who is wise, and he shall understand these things? prudent, and he shall know them? for the ways of the Lord are right, and the just shall walk in them: but the transgressors shall fall therein (Hos. 14:9).

GOD'S PROMISE FOR TODAY

The simple believeth every word; but the prudent man looketh well to his going (Prov. 14:15).

"We must be winsome to win some to Christ."

SEPTEMBER 3

Also, that the soul be without knowledge, it is not good; and he that hasteth with his feet sinneth (Prov. 19:2).

The thoughts of the diligent tend only to plenteousness; but of every one that is hasty only to want (Prov. 21:5).

Be not rash with thy mouth, and let not thine heart be hasty to utter any thing before God: for God is in heaven, and thou upon earth: therefore let thy words be few (Eccles 5:2).

Seeing then that these things cannot be spoken against, ye ought to be quiet, and to do nothing rashly (Acts 19:36).

Wherefore do ye spend money for that which is not bread? and your labour for that which satisfieth not? hearken diligently unto me, and eat ye that which is good, and let your soul delight itself in fatness (Isa. 55:2).

GOD'S PROMISE FOR TODAY

Seest thou a man that is hasty in his words? there is more hope of a fool than of him (Prov. 29:20).

"No one is useless in this world who lightens the burdens of others."

SEPTEMBER 4

When He giveth quietness, who then can make trouble? and when He hideth His face, who then can behold Him? whether it be done against a nation, or against a man only (Job 34:29).

Surely I have behaved and quieted myself, as a child that is weaned of his mother: my soul is even as a weaned child (Ps. 131:2).

But whoso hearkeneth unto Me shall dwell safely, and shall be quiet from fear of evil (Prov. 1:33).

And the work of righteousness shall be peace; and the effect of righteousness, quietness and assurance for ever (Isa. 32:17).

Be merciful unto me, O God, be merciful unto me: for my soul trusteth in Thee: yea, in the shadow of Thy wings will I make my refuge, until these calamities be overpast (Ps. 57:1).

GOD'S PROMISE FOR TODAY

Thou wilt keep him in perfect peace, whose mind is stayed on Thee: because he trusteth in Thee. Trust ye in the Lord for ever: for in the Lord Jehovah is everlasting strength (Isa. 26:3, 4).

"A wound from the tongue is worse than a wound from the sword."

SEPTEMBER 5

Better is a dry morsel, and quietness therewith, than a house full of sacrifices with strife (Prov. 17:1).

Better is a handful with quietness, than both the hands full with travail and vexation of spirit (Eccles. 4:6).

For kings, and for all that are in authority; that we may lead a quiet and peaceable life in all godliness and honesty (I Tim. 2:2).

But let it be the hidden man of the heart, in that which is not corruptible, even the ornament of a meek and quiet spirit, which is in the sight of God of great price (I Peter 3:4).

He shall be great, and shall be called the Son of the Highest; and the Lord God shall give unto Him the throne of His father David. And He shall reign over the house of Jacob for ever; and of His kingdom there shall be no end (Luke 1:32, 33).

GOD'S PROMISE FOR TODAY

And that ye study to be quiet, and to do your own business, and to work with your own hands, as we commanded you (I Thess. 4:11).

"To get the best of an argument, stay out of it."

SEPTEMBER 6

And Moses said unto them, Stand still, and I will hear what the Lord will command concerning you (Num. 9:8).

And as they were going down to the end of the city, Samuel said to Saul, Bid the servant pass on before us, (and he passed on,) but stand thou still a while, that I may shew thee the word of God (I Sam. 9:27).

Now therefore stand still, that I may reason with you before the Lord of all the righteous acts of the Lord, which He did to you and to your fathers (I Sam. 12:7).

Hearken unto this, O Job: stand still, and consider the wondrous works of God (Job 37:14).

Stand in awe, and sin not: commune with your own heart upon your bed, and be still. Selah (Ps. 4:4).

GOD'S PROMISE FOR TODAY

Be still, and know that I am God: I will be exalted among the heathen, I will be exalted in the earth (Ps. 46:10).

"The bow too tensely strung is easily broken."

SEPTEMBER 7

In those days was Hezekiah sick unto death. And the prophet Isaiah the son of Amoz came to him, and said unto him, thus saith the Lord, Set thine house in order; for thou shalt die, and not live (II Kings 20:1).

And while they went to buy, the bridegroom came; and they that were ready went in with Him to the marriage: and the door was shut (Matt. 25:10).

Let your loins be girded about, and your lights burning; and ye yourselves like unto men that wait for their lord, when he will return from the wedding (Luke 12:35, 36).

Let us be glad and rejoice, and give honour to Him: for the marriage of the Lamb is come, and His wife hath made herself ready (Rev. 19:7).

GOD'S PROMISE FOR TODAY

Therefore be ye also ready: for in such an hour as ye think not the Son of man cometh (Matt. 24:44).

"Some people never change their opinion because it has been in the family for generations."

SEPTEMBER 8

For as in the days that were before the flood they were eating and drinking, marrying and giving in marriage, until the day that Noe entered into the ark. And knew not until the flood came, and took them all away; so shall also the coming of the Son of man be (Matt. 24:38, 39).

But and if that evil servant shall say in his heart, my lord delayeth his coming; and shall begin to smite his fellow servants, and to eat and drink with the drunken; the lord of that servant shall come in a day when he looketh not for him and in an hour that he is not aware of. And shall cut him asunder, and appoint him his portion with the hypocrites: there shall be weeping and gnashing of teeth (Matt. 24:48-51).

GOD'S PROMISE FOR TODAY

For man also knoweth not his time: as the fishes that are taken in an evil net, and as the birds that are caught in the snare; so are the sons of men snared in an evil time, when it falleth suddenly upon them (Eccles. 9:12).

"A journey of a thousand miles begins with one step."

SEPTEMBER 9

And at midnight there was a cry made, Behold, the bridegroom cometh; go ye out to meet him. Then all those virgins arose, and trimmed their lamps. And the foolish said unto the wise, give us of your oil; for our lamps are gone out. But the wise answered, saying, not so; lest there be not enough for us and you: but go ye rather to them that sell, and buy for yourselves. And while they went to buy, the bridegroom came; and they that were ready went in with him to the marriage: and the door was shut (Matt. 25:6-10).

Watch ye therefore: for ye know not when the master of the house cometh, at even, or at midnight, or at the cock-crowing, or in the morning (Mark 13:35).

For as a snare shall it come on all them that dwell on the face of the whole earth (Luke 21:35).

GOD'S PROMISE FOR TODAY

And take heed to yourselves, lest at any time your hearts be overcharged with surfeiting, and drunkenness, and cares of this life, and so that day come upon you unawares (Luke 21:34).

"Behavior is a mirror in which everyone shows his image."

SEPTEMBER 10

Let us hear the conclusion of the whole matter: fear God, and keep His commandments: for this is the whole duty of man (Eccles. 12:13).

For I desired mercy, and not sacrifice; and the knowledge of God more than burnt offerings (Hos. 6:6).

He hath shewed thee, O man, what is good: and what doth the Lord require of thee, but to do justly, and to love mercy, and to walk humbly with thy God? (Mic. 6:8).

And to love Him with all the heart, and with all the understanding, and with all the soul, and with all the strength, and to love his neighbour as himself, is more than all whole burnt offerings and sacrifices (Mark 12:33).

Pure religion and undefiled before God and the Father is this, to visit the fatherless and widows in their affliction, and to keep himself unspotted from the world (James 1:27).

GOD'S PROMISE FOR TODAY

Love worketh no ill to his neighbour: therefore love is the fulfilling of the law (Rom. 13:10).

"The Lord's day is the golden clasp that binds together the volume of the week."

SEPTEMBER 11

And Samuel said, Hath the Lord as great delight in burnt offerings and sacrifices, as in obeying the voice of the Lord? Behold, to obey is better than sacrifice, and to hearken than that the fat of rams (I Sam. 15:22).

For Thou desirest not sacrifice; else would I give it: Thou delightest not in burnt offering. The sacrifices of God are a broken spirit: a broken and a contrite heart, O God, Thou wilt not despise (Ps. 51:16, 17).

Keep thy foot when thou goest to the house of God, and be more ready to hear, than to give the sacrifice of fools: for they consider not that they do evil (Eccles. 5:1).

For I desired mercy, and not sacrifice; and the knowledge of God more than burnt offerings (Hos. 6:6).

GOD'S PROMISE FOR TODAY

For the kingdom of God is not meat and drink: but righteousness, and peace, and joy in the Holy Ghost (Rom. 14:17).

"True repentance consists in the heart being broken *for* sin and broken *from* sin."

SEPTEMBER 12

For I say unto you, that except your righteousness shall exceed the righteousness of the scribes and Pharisees, ye shall in no case enter into the kingdom of heaven (Matt. 5:20).

And said, verily I say unto you, Except ye be converted, and become as little children, ye shall not enter into the kingdom of heaven (Matt. 18:3).

Then Jesus said unto them Verily, verily, I say unto you, except ye eat the flesh of the Son of man, and drink His blood, ye have no life in you (John 6:53).

I said therefore unto you, that ye shall die in your sins: for if ye believe not that I am He, ye shall die in your sins (John 8:24).

Though a sinner do evil a hundred times, and his days be prolonged, yet surely I know that it shall be well with them that fear God, which fear before Him (Eccles. 8:12).

GOD'S PROMISE FOR TODAY

God is a Spirit: and they that worship Him must worship Him in spirit and in truth (John 4:24).

"Talk will react like a chicken and always come home to roost."

SEPTEMBER 13

And He said, My presence shall go with thee, and I will give thee rest (Exod. 33:14).

And I said, Oh that I had wings like a dove! for then would I fly away, and be at rest (Ps. 55:6).

To whom He said, This is the rest wherewith ye may cause the weary to rest; and this is the refreshing: yet they would not hear (Isa. 28:12).

For we which have believed do enter into rest, as He said, as I have sworn in My wrath, if they shall enter into My rest: although the works were finished from the foundation of the world (Heb. 4:3).

And I heard a voice from heaven saying unto me, Write, blessed are the dead which die in the Lord from henceforth: yea, saith the Spirit, that they may rest from their labours; and their works do follow them (Rev. 14:13).

GOD'S PROMISE FOR TODAY

Take My yoke upon you, and learn of Me; for I am meek and lowly in heart: and ye shall find rest unto your souls (Matt. 11:29).

"As you live you will die; and as you die you will live forever."

I will both lay me down in peace, and sleep: for Thou, Lord only makest me dwell in safety (Ps. 4:8).

Through the tender mercy of our God; whereby the dayspring from on high hath visited us, to give light to them that sit in darkness and in the shadow of death, to guide our feet into the way of peace (Luke 1:78, 79).

And suddenly there was with the angel a multitude of the heavenly host praising God, and saying, Glory to God in the highest, and on earth peace, good will toward men (Luke 2:13, 14).

For the kingdom of God is not meat and drink; but righteousness, and peace, and joy in the Holy Ghost (Rom. 14:17).

But the fruit of the Spirit is love, joy, peace, longsuffering, gentleness, goodness, faith, meekness, temperance: against such there is no law (Gal. 5:22, 23).

GOD'S PROMISE FOR TODAY

For to be carnally minded is death; but to be spiritually minded is life and peace (Rom. 8:6).

"Profanity is the crutch of conversational cripples."

The Lord will give strength unto His people; the Lord will bless His people with peace (Ps. 29:11).

O that thou hadst hearkened to My commandments! then had thy peace been as a river, and thy righteousness as the waves of the sea (Isa. 48:18).

Peace I leave with you, My peace I give unto you: not as the world giveth, give I unto you. Let not your heart be troubled, neither let it be afraid (John 14:27).

These things I have spoken unto you, that in Me ye might have peace. In the world ye shall have tribulation: but be of good cheer; I have overcome the world (John 16:33).

And the peace of God, which passeth all understanding, shall keep your hearts and minds through Christ Jesus (Phil. 4:7).

GOD'S PROMISE FOR TODAY

Great peace have they which love Thy law: and nothing shall offend them (Ps. 119:165).

"Men are naturally tempted of the devil, but an idle man positively tempts the devil."

But He was wounded for our transgressions, He was bruised for our iniquities: the chastisement of our peace was upon Him; and with His stripes we are healed (Isa. 53:5).

The word which God sent unto the children of Israel, preaching peace by Jesus Christ: (He is Lord of all) (Acts 10:36).

For He is our peace, Who hath made both one, and hath broken down the middle wall of partition between us (Eph. 2:14).

And, having made peace through the blood of His cross, by Him to reconcile all things unto Himself; by Him, I say, whether they be things in earth, or things in heaven (Col. 1:20).

Thou wilt keep him in perfect peace, whose mind is stayed on Thee: because he trusteth in Thee (Isa. 26:3).

GOD'S PROMISE FOR TODAY

Therefore being justified by faith, we have peace with God through our Lord Jesus Christ (Rom. 5:1).

> "You would be cheated if you paid a penny for
> some people's thoughts."

SEPTEMBER 17

It is vain for you to rise up early, to sit up late, to eat the bread of sorrows; for so He giveth His beloved sleep (Ps. 127:2).

Therefore I say unto you, take no thought of your life, what ye shall eat, or what ye shall drink; nor yet for your body, what ye shall put on. Is not the life more than meat, and the body more than raiment? (Matt. 6:25).

And Jesus answered and said unto her, Martha, Martha, thou art careful and troubled about many things (Luke 10:41).

And take heed to yourselves, lest at any time your hearts be overcharged with surfeiting, and drunkenness, and cares of this life, and so that day come upon you unawares (Luke 21:34).

Be careful for nothing: but in every thing by prayer and supplication with thanksgiving let your requests be made known unto God (Phil. 4:6).

GOD'S PROMISE FOR TODAY

Casting all your care upon Him; for He careth for you (I Peter 5:7).

> "Floating church members make a sinking church."

And he said, Draw not nigh hither: put off thy shoes from off thy feet; for the place whereon thou standest is holy ground (Exod. 3:5).

And the captain of the Lord's host said unto Joshua, Loose thy shoe from off thy foot; for the place whereon thou standest is holy. And Joshua did so (Josh. 5:15).

Stand in awe, and sin not: commune with your own heart upon your bed, and be still (Ps. 4:4).

Let all the earth fear the Lord: let all the inhabitants of the world stand in awe of Him (Ps. 33:8).

God is greatly to be feared in the assembly of the saints, and to be had in reverence of all them that are about Him (Ps. 89:7).

GOD'S PROMISE FOR TODAY

But the Lord is in His holy temple: let all the earth keep silence before Him (Hab. 2:20).

"Life with Christ is an endless hope; without Him it is a hopeless end."

If ye will fear the Lord and serve Him, and obey His voice, and not rebel against the commandment of the Lord; then shall both ye and also the king that reigneth over you continue following the Lord your God (I Sam. 12:14).

Oh, how great is Thy goodness, which Thou hast laid up for them that fear Thee: which Thou hast wrought for them that trust in Thee before the sons of men! (Ps. 31:19).

Who is among you that feareth the Lord, that obeyeth the voice of His servant, that walketh in darkness, and hath no light? let him trust in the name of the Lord, and stay upon his God (Isa. 50:10).

And His mercy is on them that fear Him from generation to generation (Luke 1:50).

But in every nation he that feareth Him, and worketh righteousness, is accepted with Him (Acts 10:35).

GOD'S PROMISE FOR TODAY

What man is he that feareth the Lord? him shall He teach in the way that he shall choose (Ps. 25:12).

"The first step toward correcting a fault is to admit it."

He withdraweth not His eyes from the righteous: but with kings are they on the throne; yea, He doth establish them for ever, and they are exalted (Job 36:7).

The eyes of the Lord are upon the righteous, and His ears are open unto their cry (Ps. 34:15).

The righteous shall flourish like a palm tree: he shall grow like a cedar in Lebanon (Ps. 92:12).

Say ye to the righteous, that it shall be well with him: for they shall eat the fruit of their doings (Isa. 3:10).

Then shall the righteous shine forth as the sun in the kingdom of their Father. Who hath ears to hear, let him hear (Matt. 13:43).

Return unto thy rest, O my soul: for the Lord hath dealt bountifully with thee (Ps. 116:7).

GOD'S PROMISE FOR TODAY

I have been young, and now am old; yet have I not seen the righteous forsaken, nor His seed begging bread (Ps. 37:25).

"The less thunder, the gentler the rainfall."

I exhort therefore, that, first of all, supplications, prayers, intercessions, and giving of thanks, be made for all men; for kings, and for all that are in authority; that we may lead a quiet and peaceable life in all godliness and honesty (I Tim. 2:1, 2).

But refuse profane and old wives' fables, and exercise thyself rather unto godliness (I Tim. 4:7).

Teaching us that, denying ungodliness and worldly lusts, we should live soberly, righteously, and godly, in this present world (Titus 2:12).

Seeing then that all these things shall be dissolved, what manner of persons ought ye to be in all holy conversation and godliness (II Peter 3:11).

GOD'S PROMISE FOR TODAY

But thou, O man of God, flee these things; and follow after righteousness, godliness, faith, love, patience, meekness (I Tim. 6:11).

"You cannot build a reputation on things you are going to do."

But the salvation of the righteous is of the Lord: He is their strength in the time of trouble (Ps. 37:39).

Behold, God is my salvation; I will trust, and not be afraid: for the Lord Jehovah is my strength and my song; He also is become my salvation (Isa. 12:2).

And it shall be said in that day, Lo, this is our God; we have waited for Him, and He will save us: this is the Lord; we have waited for Him, we will be glad and rejoice in His salvation (Isa. 25:9).

The Lord thy God in the midst of thee is mighty; He will save, He will rejoice over thee with joy; He will rest in His love, He will joy over thee with singing (Zeph. 3:17).

GOD'S PROMISE FOR TODAY

The Lord is my light and my salvation; whom shall I fear? the Lord is the strength of my life; of whom shall I be afraid? (Ps. 27:1).

> "Life is not so short but that there is always time for courtesy."

And ye shall be hated of all men for My name's sake: but he that endureth to the end shall be saved (Matt. 10:22).

Wherefore lay apart all filthiness and superfluity of naughtiness, and receive with meekness the engrafted word, which is able to save your souls (James 1:21).

Wherefore the rather, brethren, give diligence to make your calling and election sure: for if ye do these things, ye shall never fall: for so an entrance shall be ministered unto you abundantly into the everlasting kingdom of our Lord and Saviour Jesus Christ (II Peter 1:10, 11).

Blessed are they that wash their robes, that they may have the right to come to the tree of life, and may enter in by the gates into the city (Rev. 22:14, RV).

GOD'S PROMISE FOR TODAY

That if thou shalt confess with thy mouth the Lord Jesus, and shalt believe in thine heart that God hath raised Him from the dead, thou shalt be saved (Rom. 10:9).

> "Man's best possession is a sympathetic wife."

And all flesh shall see the salvation of God (Luke 3:6).

Therefore, as by the offence of one judgment came upon all men to condemnation; even so by the righteousness of One the free gift came upon all men unto justification of life (Rom. 5:18).

For whosoever shall call upon the name of the Lord shall be saved (Rom. 10:13).

For the grace of God that bringeth salvation hath appeared to all men, teaching us that, denying ungodliness and worldly lusts, we should live soberly, righteously, and godly, in this present world (Titus 2:11, 12).

The Lord is not slack concerning His promise, as some men count slackness; but is longsuffering to us-ward, not willing that any should perish, but that all should come to repentance (II Peter 3:9).

GOD'S PROMISE FOR TODAY

And it shall come to pass, that whosoever shall call on the name of the Lord shall be saved (Acts 2:21).

"Prosperity makes friends, adversity tries them."

For God so loved the world, that He gave His only begotten Son, that whosoever believeth in Him should not perish, but have everlasting life (John 3:16).

Jesus answered and said unto her, if thou knewest the gift of God, and Who it is that saith to thee, give Me to drink; thou wouldest have asked of Him, and He would have given thee living water (John 4:10).

For the wages of sin is death; but the gift of God is eternal life through Jesus Christ our Lord (Rom. 6:23).

He that spared not His own Son, but delivered Him up for us all, how shall He not with Him also freely give us all things? (Rom. 8:32).

Thanks be unto God for His unspeakable gift (II Cor. 9:15).

Who will have all men to be saved, and to come unto the knowledge of the truth (I Tim. 2:4).

GOD'S PROMISE FOR TODAY

For by grace are ye saved through faith; and that not of yourselves: it is the gift of God (Eph. 2:8).

"Some are wise, and some are otherwise."

Behold, the Lord God will help me; who is he that shall condemn me? lo, they all shall wax old as a garment; the moth shall eat them up (Isa. 50:9).

He that believeth on Him is not condemned: but he that believeth not is condemned already, because he hath not believed in the name of the only begotten Son of God (John 3:18).

Verily, verily, I say unto you, He that heareth My word, and believeth on Him that sent Me, hath everlasting life, and shall not come into condemnation; but is passed from death unto life (John 5:24).

Who is he that condemneth? It is Christ that died, yea rather, that is risen again, Who is even at the right hand of God, Who also maketh intercession for us (Rom. 8:34).

GOD'S PROMISE FOR TODAY

There is therefore now no condemnation to them which are in Christ Jesus, who walk not after the flesh, but after the Spirit (Rom. 8:1).

"It is not enough to be busy; so are the ants. The question is: What are we busy about?"

I, even I, am He that blotteth out thy transgressions for mine own sake, and will not remember thy sins (Isa. 43:25).

I have blotted out, as a thick cloud, thy transgressions, and, as a cloud, thy sins: return unto me; for I have redeemed thee (Isa. 44:22).

Let the wicked forsake his way, and the unrighteous man his thoughts: and let him return unto the Lord, and He will have mercy upon him; and to our God, for He will abundantly pardon (Isa. 55:7).

Who is a God like unto Thee, that pardoneth iniquity, and passeth by the transgression of the remnant of His heritage? He retaineth not His anger for ever, because He delighteth in mercy (Mic. 7:18).

GOD'S PROMISE FOR TODAY

If we confess our sins, He is faithful and just to forgive us our sins, and to cleanse us from all unrighteousness (I John 1:9).

"He is happiest, be he king or peasant, who finds peace in his home."

For this is My blood of the new testament, which is shed for many for the remission of sins (Matt. 26:28).

And He came into all the country about Jordan, preaching the baptism of repentance for the remission of sins (Luke 3:3).

And that repentance and remission of sins should be preached in His name among all nations, beginning at Jerusalem (Luke 24:47).

Now before the feast of the passover, when Jesus knew that His hour was come that He should depart out of this world unto the Father, having loved His own which were in the world, He loved them unto the end (John 13:1).

Then Peter said unto them, repent, and be baptized every one of you in the name of Jesus Christ for the remission of sins, and ye shall receive the gift of the Holy Ghost (Acts 2:38).

GOD'S PROMISE FOR TODAY

And almost all things are by the law purged with blood; and without shedding of blood is no remission (Heb. 9:22).

"True men are cheerful in distress."

SEPTEMBER 29

Go ye, inquire of the Lord for me, and for the people, and for all Judah, concerning the words of this book that is found: for great is the wrath of the Lord that is kindled against us, because our fathers have not hearkened unto the words of this book, to do according unto all that which is written concerning us (II Kings 22:13).

For the wrath of God is revealed from heaven against all ungodliness and unrighteousness of men, who hold the truth in unrighteousness (Rom. 1:18).

But unto them that are contentious, and do not obey the truth, but obey unrighteousness, indignation and wrath (Rom. 2:8).

Let no man deceive you with vain words: for because of these things cometh the wrath of God upon the children of disobedience (Eph. 5:6).

GOD'S PROMISE FOR TODAY

Kiss the Son, lest He be angry, and ye perish from the way, when His wrath is kindled but a little. Blessed are all they that put their trust in Him (Ps. 2:12).

"Forethought is better than repentance."

Sanctify them through Thy truth: Thy word is truth (John 17:17).

But of Him are ye in Christ Jesus, Who of God is made unto us wisdom, and rightousness, and sanctification, and redemption (I Cor. 1:30).

That He might sanctify and cleanse it with the washing of water by the word (Eph. 5:26).

Wherefore Jesus also, that He might sanctify the people with His own blood, suffered without the gate (Heb. 13:12).

Elect according to the foreknowledge of God the Father, through sanctification of the Spirit, unto obedience and sprinkling of the blood of Jesus Christ: grace unto you, and peace, be multiplied (I Peter 1:2).

GOD'S PROMISE FOR TODAY

If a man therefore purge himself from these, he shall be a vessel unto honour, sanctified, and meet for the master's use, and prepared unto every good work (II Tim. 2:21).

"An empty man is full of himself."

October

OCTOBER 1

Be ye angry, and sin not; let not the sun go down upon your wrath: neither give place to the devil (Eph. 4:26, 27).

Put on the whole armour of God, that ye may be able to stand against the wiles of the devil (Eph. 6:11).

Be sober, be watchful: your adversary the devil, as a roaring lion, walketh about, seeking whom he may devour: whom withstand stedfast in your faith, knowing that the same sufferings are accomplished in your brethren who are in the world (I Peter 5:8, 9, RV).

Judge not, and ye shall not be judged: condemn not, and ye shall not be condemned: forgive, and ye shall be forgiven (Luke 6:37).

And seek not ye what ye shall eat, or what ye shall drink, neither be ye of doubtful mind (Luke 12:29).

GOD'S PROMISE FOR TODAY

Submit yourselves therefore to God. Resist the devil, and he will flee from you (James 4:7).

"The gossiper is like an old shoe on which the tongue never stays in place."

OCTOBER 2

And thou shalt be secure, because there is hope; yea, thou shalt dig about thee, and thou shalt take thy rest in safety (Job 11:18).

Thou shalt not be afraid for the terror by night; nor for the arrow that flieth by day (Ps. 91:5).

When thou liest down, thou shalt not be afraid: yea, thou shalt lie down, and thy sleep shall be sweet (Prov. 3:24).

So that we may boldly say, The Lord is my helper, and I will not fear what man shall do unto me (Heb. 13:6).

And who is he that will harm you, if ye be followers of that which is good? (I Peter 3:13).

GOD'S PROMISE FOR TODAY

He shall not be afraid of evil tidings: his heart is fixed, trusting in the Lord (Ps. 112:7).

"Our eyes are placed in front because it is more important to look ahead than to look back."

OCTOBER 3

Therefore thus saith the Lord God, behold, I lay in Zion for a foundation a stone, a tried stone, a precious corner stone, a sure foundation: he that believeth shall not make haste (Isa. 28:16).

Therefore whosoever heareth these sayings of Mine, and doeth them, I will liken him unto a wise man, which built his house upon a rock (Matt. 7:24).

Laying up in store for themselves a good foundation against the time to come, that they may lay hold on eternal life (I Tim. 6:19).

Nevertheless the foundation of God standeth sure, having this seal, the Lord knoweth them that are His, and, let every one that nameth the name of Christ depart from iniquity (II Tim. 2:19).

GOD'S PROMISE FOR TODAY

For other foundation can no man lay than that is laid, which is Jesus Christ (I Cor. 3:11).

"Who learns and learns, and acts not what he knows, is like one who plows and plows, but never sows."

OCTOBER 4

Cease ye from man, whose breath is in his nostrils: for wherein is he to be accounted of? (Isa. 2:22).

Woe to them that go down to Egypt for help; and stay on horses, and trust in chariots, because they are many; and in horsemen, because they are very strong; but they look not unto the Holy One of Israel, neither seek the Lord (Isa. 31:1).

Thus saith the Lord; Cursed be the man that trusteth in man, and maketh flesh his arm, and whose heart departeth from the Lord (Jer. 17:5).

There is that maketh himself rich, yet hath nothing: there is that maketh himself poor, yet hath great riches (Prov. 13:7).

And I will say to my soul, Soul, thou hast much goods laid up for many years: take thine ease, eat, drink, and be merry (Luke 12:19).

GOD'S PROMISE FOR TODAY

It is better to trust in the Lord than to put confidence in princes (Ps. 118:9).

"In essentials unity. In *non-essentials* freedom. In *all things* love."*

OCTOBER 5

Lo, this is the man that made not God his strength; but trusted in the abundance of his riches, and strengthened himself in his wickedness (Ps. 52:7).

The rich man's wealth is his strong city, and as a high wall in his own conceit (Prov. 18:11).

And the disciples were astonished at His words. But Jesus answered again, and saith unto them, Children, how hard is it for them that trust in riches to enter into the kingdom of God! (Mark 10:24).

And I will say to my soul, Soul, thou hast much goods laid up for many years: take thine ease, eat, drink and be merry. But God said unto him, Thou fool, this night thy soul shall be required of thee: then whose shall those things be, which thou hast provided? (Luke 12:19, 20).

GOD'S PROMISE FOR TODAY

Charge them that are rich in this world, that they be not high-minded, nor trust in uncertain riches, but in the living God, Who giveth us richly all things to enjoy (I Tim. 6:17).

"Every man should keep a fair-sized cemetery in which to bury the faults of his friends."

OCTOBER 6

But if from thence thou shalt seek the Lord thy God, thou

shalt find Him, if thou seek Him with all thy heart and with all thy soul (Deut. 4:29).

Seek the Lord, and His strength: seek His face evermore (Ps. 105:4).

Sow to yourselves in righteousness, reap in mercy; break up your fallow ground: for it is time to seek the Lord, till He come and rain righteousness upon you (Hos. 10:12).

For every one that asketh receiveth; and he that seeketh findeth; and to him that knocketh it shall be opened (Luke 11:10).

That they should seek the Lord, if haply they might feel after Him, and find Him, though He be not far from every one of us (Acts 17:27).

GOD'S PROMISE FOR TODAY

Seek ye the Lord while He may be found, call ye upon Him while He is near (Isa. 55:6).

"In prayer it is better to have a heart without words, than words without heart."

OCTOBER 7

He loveth transgression that loveth strife: and he that exalteth his gate seeketh destruction (Prov. 17:19).

Put not forth thyself in the presence of the king, and stand not in the place of great men; for better it is that it be said unto thee, Come up hither; than that thou shouldest be put lower in the presence of the prince whom thine eyes have seen (Prov. 25:6, 7).

Though thou exalt thyself as the eagle, and though thou set thy nest among the stars, thence will I bring thee down, saith the Lord (Obad. vs. 4).

It is not good to eat much honey: so for men to search their own glory is not glory (Prov. 25:27).

They said unto Him, grant unto us that we may sit, one on Thy right hand, and the other on Thy left hand, in Thy glory (Mark 10:37).

GOD'S PROMISE FOR TODAY

And whosoever shall exalt himself shall be abased; and he that shall humble himself shall be exalted (Matt. 23:12).

"Some people take a stand for Christ—and never move again."

For he flattereth himself in his own eyes, until his iniquity be found to be hateful (Ps. 36:2).

He feedeth on ashes: a deceived heart hath turned him aside, that he cannot deliver his soul, nor say, Is there not a lie in my right hand? (Isa. 44:20).

But be ye doers of the word, and not hearers only, deceiving your own selves (James 1:22).

If any man among you seem to be religious, and bridleth not his tongue, but deceiveth his own heart, this man's religion is vain (James 1:26).

If we say that we have no sin, we deceive ourselves, and the truth is not in us (I John 1:8).

Because thou sayest, I am rich, and increased with goods, and have need of nothing: and knowest not that thou art wretched, and miserable, and poor, and blind, and naked (Rev. 3:17).

GOD'S PROMISE FOR TODAY

For if a man think himself to be something, when he is nothing, he deceiveth himself (Gal. 6:3).

"Some people have heaven at their tongue's tip but the world at their finger's end."

He that loveth pleasure shall be a poor man: he that loveth wine and oil shall not be rich (Prov. 21:17).

Therefore hear now this, thou that art given to pleasures, that dwellest carelessly, that sayest in thine heart, I am, and none else beside me: I shall not sit as a widow, neither shall I know the loss of children: but these two things shall come to thee in a moment in one day, the loss of children, and widowhood (Isa. 47:8, 9).

And that which fell among thorns are they, which, when they have heard, go forth, and are choked with cares and riches and pleasures of this life, and bring no fruit to perfection (Luke 8:14).

And shall receive the reward of unrighteousness, as they that count it pleasure to riot in the daytime. Spots they are and blemishes, sporting themselves with their own deceivings while they feast with you (II Peter 2:13).

But she that liveth in pleasure is dead while she liveth (I Tim. 5:6).

"You always have time for the thing you put first."

OCTOBER 10

Then said Jesus unto His disciples, If any man will come after Me, let him deny himself, and take up his cross, and follow Me (Matt. 16:24).

If any man come to Me, and hate not his father, and mother, and wife, and children, and brethren, and sisters, yea, and his own life also, he cannot be My disciple. And whosoever doth not bear his cross, and come after Me, cannot be My disciple (Luke 14:26, 27).

For if ye live after the flesh, ye shall die: but if ye through the Spirit do mortify the deeds of the body, ye shall live (Rom. 8:13).

We then that are strong ought to bear the infirmities of the weak, and not to please ourselves (Rom. 15:1).

Laying up in store for themselves a good foundation against the time to come, that they may lay hold on eternal life (I Tim. 6:19).

GOD'S PROMISE FOR TODAY

And they that are Christ's have crucified the flesh with the affections and lusts (Gal. 5:24).

"You can't have your own way unless you make God's way your way."

OCTOBER 11

Then Peter began to say unto Him, Lo, we have left all, and have followed Thee (Mark 10:28).

And after these things He went forth, and saw a publican, named Levi, sitting at the receipt of custom: and He said unto him, Follow Me. And he left all, rose up, and followed Him (Luke 5:27, 28).

And He said unto them, verily I say unto you, there is no man that hath left house, or parents, or brethren, or wife, or children, for the kingdom of God's sake, who shall not receive manifold more in this present time, and in the world to come life everlasting (Luke 18:29, 30).

Yea, doubtless, and I count all things but loss for the excellency of the knowledge of Christ Jesus my Lord: for Whom I have suffered the loss of all things, and do count them but dung, that I may win Christ (Phil. 3:8).

GOD'S PROMISE FOR TODAY

So likewise, whosoever he be of you that forsaketh not all that he hath, he cannot be My disciple (Luke 14:33).

"Give all He asks; take all He gives; and your cup will be spilling joyously over the brim."

OCTOBER 12

When thou sittest to eat with a ruler, consider diligently what is before thee (Prov. 23:1).

Be not among winebibbers; among riotous eaters of flesh (Prov. 23:20).

And He said unto His disciples, therefore I say unto you, take no thought for your life, what ye shall eat; neither for the body, what ye shall put on (Luke 12:22).

And put a knife to thy throat, if thou be a man given to appetite (Prov. 23:2).

And take heed to yourselves, lest at any time your hearts be overcharged with surfeiting, and drunkenness, and cares of this life, and so that day come upon you unawares (Luke 21:34).

But I keep under my body, and bring it into subjection: lest that by any means, when I have preached to others, I myself should be a castaway (I Cor. 9:27).

GOD'S PROMISE FOR TODAY

But the rich, in that he is made low; because as the flower of the grass he shall pass away (James 1:10).

"It is easy to give your major attention to minor matters."

OCTOBER 13

And if thy right eye offend thee, pluck it out, and cast it from thee: for it is profitable for thee that one of thy members should perish, and not that thy whole body should be cast into hell (Matt. 5:29).

Knowing this, that our old man is crucified with Him, that the body of sin might be destroyed, that henceforth, we should not serve sin (Rom. 6:6).

But put ye on the Lord Jesus Christ, and make not provision for the flesh, to fulfil the lusts thereof (Rom. 13:14).

Mortify therefore your members which are upon the earth; fornication, uncleanness, inordinate affection, evil concupiscence, and covetousness, which is idolatry (Col. 3:5).

That he no longer should live the rest of his time in the flesh to the lusts of men, but to the will of God (I Peter 4:2).

GOD'S PROMISE FOR TODAY

This I say then, walk in the Spirit, and ye shall not fulfil the lust of the flesh (Gal. 5:16).

"People who get something for nothing usually kick about the quality of it."

OCTOBER 14

It is good neither to eat flesh, nor to drink wine, nor any thing whereby thy brother stumbleth, or is offended, or is made weak (Rom. 14:21).

Jesus said unto him, if thou wilt be perfect, go and sell that thou hast, and give to the poor, and thou shalt have treasure in heaven: and come and follow Me (Matt. 19:21).

Let no man seek his own, but every man another's wealth (I Cor. 10:24).

Look not every man on his own things, but every man also on the things of others (Phil. 2:4).

Wherefore in all things it behooved Him to be made like unto His brethren, that He might be a merciful and faithful high priest in things pertaining to God, to make reconciliation for the sins of the people (Heb. 2:17).

GOD'S PROMISE FOR TODAY

For whosoever will save his life shall lose it: and whosoever will lose his life for My sake shall find it (Matt. 16:25).

"Diplomacy: The art of letting someone else have their own way."

OCTOBER 15

The Lord is my shepherd; I shall not want. He maketh me to lie down in green pastures: He leadeth me beside the still waters (Ps. 23:1, 2).

He shall feed His flock like a shepherd: He shall gather the lambs with His arm, and carry them in His bosom, and shall gently lead those that are with young (Isa. 40:11).

I am the good Shepherd: the good shepherd giveth His life for the sheep (John 10:11).

Now the God of peace, that brought again from the dead our Lord Jesus, that great Shepherd of the sheep, through the blood of the everlasting covenant (Heb. 13:20).

For ye were as sheep going astray; but are now returned unto the Shepherd and Bishop of your souls (I Peter 2:25).

GOD'S PROMISE FOR TODAY

And when the chief Shepherd shall appear, ye shall receive a crown of glory that fadeth not away (I Peter 5:4).

"Learn from the mistakes of others—you can't live long enough to make them all yourself."

OCTOBER 16

My people hath been lost sheep: their shepherds have caused them to go astray, they have turned them away on the mountains: they have gone from mountain to hill, they have forgotten their resting place (Jer. 50:6).

My sheep wandered through all the mountains, and upon every high hill: yea, My flock was scattered upon all the face of the earth, and none did search or seek after them (Ezek. 34:6).

But when He saw the multitudes, He was moved with compassion on them, because they fainted, and were scattered abroad, as sheep having no shepherd (Matt. 9:36).

But He answered and said, I am not sent but unto the lost sheep of the house of Israel (Matt. 15:24).

GOD'S PROMISE FOR TODAY

How think ye? if a man have a hundred sheep, and one of them be gone astray, doth he not leave the ninety and nine, and goeth into the mountains, and seeketh that which is gone astray? (Matt. 18:12).

"Many treat their religion as a spare tire—they never use it except in an emergency."

OCTOBER 17

He that hath knowledge spareth his words: and a man of understanding is of an excellent spirit (Prov. 17:27).

But let your communication be, yea, yea; nay, nay: for whatsoever is more than these cometh of evil (Matt. 5:37).

Hold fast the form of sound words, which thou hast heard of me, in faith and love which is in Christ Jesus (II Tim. 1:13).

Sound speech, that cannot be condemned; that he that is of the contrary part may be ashamed, having no evil thing to say of you (Titus 2:8).

For in many things we offend all. If any man offend not in word, the same is a perfect man, and able also to bridle the whole body (James 3:2).

GOD'S PROMISE FOR TODAY

Let your speech be always with grace, seasoned with salt, that ye may know how ye ought to answer every man (Col. 4:6).

"All the man-made keys in the world cannot unlock true happiness."

OCTOBER 18

Pleasant words are as a honeycomb, sweet to the soul, and health to the bones (Prov. 16:24).

A word fitly spoken is like apples of gold in pictures of silver (Prov. 25:11).

The words of a wise man's mouth are gracious; but the lips of a fool will swallow up himself (Eccles. 10:12).

The Lord God hath given me the tongue of the learned, that I should know how to speak a word in season to him that is weary: he wakeneth morning by morning, he wakeneth mine ear to hear as the learned (Isa. 50:4).

But now I have written unto you not to keep company, if any man that is called a brother be a fornicator, or covetous, or an idolater, or a railer, or a drunkard, or an extortioner; with such a one no not to eat (I Cor. 5:11).

GOD'S PROMISE FOR TODAY

How forcible are right words! (Job 6:25).

"It is much easier to be critical than to be correct."

OCTOBER 19

And thou shalt teach them diligently unto thy children and shalt talk of them when thou sittest in thine house, and when thou walkest by the way, and when thou liest down, and when thou risest up (Deut. 6:7).

They shall speak of the glory of Thy kingdom, and talk of Thy power (Ps. 145:11).

And, behold, two of them went that same day to a village called Emmaus, which was from Jerusalem about threescore furlongs.

And they talked together of all these things which had happened (Luke 24:13, 14).

And they said one to another, did not our heart burn within us, while He talked with us by the way, and while He opened to us the Scriptures? (Luke 24:32).

GOD'S PROMISE FOR TODAY

Speaking to yourselves in psalms and hymns and spiritual songs, singing and making melody in your heart to the Lord (Eph. 5:19).

"Love is its own reward; hate its own punishment."

OCTOBER 20

Put them in mind to be subject to principalities and powers, to obey magistrates, to be ready to every good work, to speak evil of no man, to be no brawlers, but gentle, shewing all meekness unto all men (Titus 3:1, 2).

And the tongue is a fire, a world of iniquity: so is the tongue among our members, that it defileth the whole body, and setteth on fire the course of nature; and it is set on fire of hell (James 3:6).

Speak not evil one of another, brethren. He that speaketh evil of his brother, and judgeth his brother, speaketh evil of the law, and judgeth the law: but if thou judge the law, thou are not a doer of the law, but a judge (James 4:11).

Wherefore laying aside all malice, and all guile, and hypocrisies, and envies, and all evil speakings (I Peter 2:1).

GOD'S PROMISE FOR TODAY

Let all bitterness, and wrath, and anger, and clamour, and evil speaking, be put away from you, with all malice (Eph. 4:31).

"Unless there is within us that which is above us, we will soon yield to that which is about us."

OCTOBER 21

Keep thy tongue from evil and thy lips from speaking guile (Ps. 34:13).

He that keepeth his mouth keepeth his life: but he that openeth wide his lips shall have destruction (Prov. 13:3).

Whoso keepeth his mouth and his tongue, keepeth his soul from troubles (Prov. 21:23).

For he that will love life, and see good days, let him refrain his tongue from evil, and his lips that they speak no guile (I Peter 3:10).

Then they that feared the Lord spake often one to another: and the Lord hearkened, and heard it, and a book of remembrance was written before Him for them that feared the Lord, and that thought upon His name (Mal. 3:16).

GOD'S PROMISE FOR TODAY

If any man among you seem to be religious, and bridleth not his tongue, but deceiveth his own heart, this man's religion is vain (James 1:26).

"All my life's 'why's' and 'when's' and 'where's' and 'where-fore's' are in God's hands."

OCTOBER 22

Surely I have behaved and quieted myself, as a child that is weaned of his mother: my soul is even as a weaned child (Ps. 131:2).

Verily I say unto you, Whosoever shall not receive the kingdom of God as a little child, he shall not enter therein (Mark 10:15).

But Jesus called them unto Him, and said, Suffer little children to come unto Me, and forbid them not: for of such is the kingdom of God (Luke 18:16).

As newborn babes, desire the sincere milk of the word, that ye may grow thereby (I Peter 2:2).

GOD'S PROMISE FOR TODAY

Brethren, be not children in understanding: howbeit in malice be ye children, but in understanding be men (I Cor. 14:20).

"Men are used as they use others."

OCTOBER 23

In the multitude of words there wanteth not sin: but he that refraineth his lips is wise (Prov. 10:19).

He that despiseth his neighbor sinneth: but he that hath mercy on the poor, happy is he (Prov. 14:21).

The thought of foolishness is sin: and the scorner is an abomination to men (Prov. 24:9).

And he that doubteth is damned if he eat, because he eateth not of faith: for whatsoever is not of faith is sin (Rom. 14:23).

Whosoever committeth sin transgresseth also the law: for sin is the transgression of the law (I John 3:4).

All unrighteousness is sin: and there is a sin not unto death (I John 5:17).

For it is a shame even to speak of those things which are done of them in secret (Eph. 5:12).

GOD'S PROMISE FOR TODAY

Therefore to him that knoweth to do good, and doeth it not, to him it is sin (James 4:17).

"Second thoughts are ever wiser."

OCTOBER 24

Wash you, make you clean; put away the evil of your doings from before Mine eyes; cease to do evil (Isa. 1:16).

Afterward Jesus findeth him in the temple, and said unto him, Behold, thou art made whole: sin no more, lest a worse thing come unto thee (John 5:14).

She said, No man, Lord. And Jesus said unto her, Neither do I condemn thee: go, and sin no more (John 8:11).

Awake to righteousness, and sin not; for some have not the knowledge of God: I speak this to your shame (I Cor. 15:34).

Dearly beloved, I beseech you as strangers and pilgrims, abstain from fleshly lusts, which war against the soul (I Peter 2:11).

For our light affliction, which is but for a moment, worketh for us a far more exceeding and eternal weight of glory (II Cor. 4:17).

GOD'S PROMISE FOR TODAY

Let not sin therefore reign in your mortal body, that ye should obey it in the lusts thereof (Rom. 6:12).

"Hasty climbers have sudden falls."

OCTOBER 25

If iniquity be in thine hand, put it far away, and let not wickedness dwell in thy tabernacles (Job 11:14).

Let the wicked forsake his way, and the unrighteous man his thoughts: and let him return unto the Lord, and He will have mercy upon him; and to our God, for He will abundantly pardon (Isa. 55:7).

That ye put off concerning the former conversation the old man, which is corrupt according to the deceitful lusts (Eph. 4:22).

Wherefore, seeing we also are compassed about with so great a cloud of witnesses, let us lay aside every weight, and the sin which doth so easily beset us, and let us run with patience the race that is set before us (Heb. 12:1).

GOD'S PROMISE FOR TODAY

Dearly beloved, I beseech you as strangers and pilgrims, abstain from fleshly lusts, which war against the soul (I Peter 2:11).

"The man who rows a boat generally doesn't have time to rock it."

OCTOBER 26

For unto you is born this day in the city of David a Saviour, which is Christ the Lord (Luke 2:11).

For the Son of man is come to seek and to save that which was lost (Luke 19:10).

Him hath God exalted with His right hand to be a Prince and a Saviour, for to give repentance to Israel, and forgiveness of sins (Acts 5:31).

This is a faithful saying, and worthy of all acceptation, that Christ Jesus came into the world to save sinners, of whom I am chief (I Tim. 1:15).

Wherefore He is able also to save them to the uttermost that come unto God by Him, seeing He ever liveth to make intercession for them (Heb. 7:25).

GOD'S PROMISE FOR TODAY

For God sent not His Son into the world to condemn the world; but that the world through Him might be saved (John 3:17).

"What we weave on earth we will wear in heaven."

OCTOBER 27

For the zeal of thine house hath eaten Me up; and the reproaches of them that reproached thee are fallen upon Me (Ps. 69:9).

Christ hath redeemed us from the curse of the law, being made a curse for us: for it is written, cursed is every one that hangeth on a tree (Gal. 3:13).

But we see Jesus, Who was made a little lower than the angels for the suffering of death, crowned with glory and honour;

that He by the grace of God should taste death for every man (Heb. 2:9).

For Christ also hath once suffered for sins, the just for the unjust, that He might bring us to God, being put to death in the flesh, but quickened by the Spirit (I Peter 3:18).

GOD'S PROMISE FOR TODAY

But He was wounded for our transgressions, He was bruised for our iniquities: the chastisement of our peace was upon Him; and with His stripes we are healed (Isa. 53:5).

"He who much has suffered, much will know."

OCTOBER 28

He was oppressed, and He was afflicted, yet He opened not His mouth: He is brought as a lamb to the slaughter, and as a sheep before her shearers is dumb, so He openeth not His mouth (Isa. 53:7).

Purge out therefore the old leaven, that ye may be a new lump, as ye are unleavened. For even Christ our passover is sacrificed for us (I Cor. 5:7).

But with the precious blood of Christ, as of a lamb without blemish and without spot (I Peter 1:19).

After this I beheld, and, lo, a great multitude, which no man could number, of all nations, and kindreds, and people, and tongues, stood before the throne, and before the Lamb, clothed with white robes, and palms in their hands (Rev. 7:9).

And I saw no temple therein: for the Lord God Almighty and the Lamb are the temple of it (Rev. 21:22).

GOD'S PROMISE FOR TODAY

The next day John seeth Jesus coming unto him, and saith, Behold the Lamb of God, which taketh away the sin of the world! (John 1:29).

"The heir of heaven need envy no one."

OCTOBER 29

Greater love hath no man than this, that a man lay down his life for his friends (John 15:13).

Who gave Himself for our sins, that He might deliver us from this present evil world, according to the will of God and our Father (Gal. 1:4).

And walk in love, as Christ also hath loved us, and hath given

Himself for us an offering and a sacrifice to God for a sweet-smelling savour (Eph. 5:2).

Hereby perceive we the love of God, because He laid down His life for us; and we ought to lay down our lives for the brethren (I John 3:16).

And from Jesus Christ, Who is the faithful witness, and the first begotten of the dead, and the prince of the kings of the earth. Unto Him that loved us, and washed us from our sins in His own blood (Rev. 1:5).

GOD'S PROMISE FOR TODAY

Who gave Himself for us, that He might redeem us from all iniquity, and purify unto Himself a peculiar people, zealous of good works (Titus 2:14).

"How rare it is to find a soul quiet enough to hear God speak."

OCTOBER 30

And He saw there was no man, and wondered that there was no intercessor: therefore His arm brought salvation unto him; and His righteousness, it sustained him (Isa. 59:16).

And as Moses lifted up the serpent in the wilderness, even so must the Son of man be lifted up: that whosoever believeth in Him should not perish, but have eternal life (John 3:14, 15).

And Jesus said unto them, I am the bread of life: he that cometh to Me shall never hunger; and he that believeth on Me shall never thirst (John 6:35).

Will ye also go away? Then Simon Peter answered Him, Lord, to whom shall we go? Thou hast the words of eternal life (John 6:67, 68).

For other foundation can no man lay than that is laid, which is Jesus Christ (I Cor. 3:11).

GOD'S PROMISE FOR TODAY

Neither is there salvation in any other: for there is none other name under heaven given among men, whereby we must be saved (Acts 4:12).

"You haven't begun to give until you rejoice over it."

OCTOBER 31

I laid me down and slept; I awaked; for the Lord sustained me (Ps. 3:5).

I will both lay me down in peace, and sleep: for Thou, Lord, only makest me dwell in safety (Ps. 4:8).

When thou liest down, thou shalt not be afraid: yea, thou shalt lie down, and thy sleep shall be sweet (Prov. 3:24).

Upon this I awaked, and beheld; and my sleep was sweet unto me (Jer. 31:26).

Give not sleep to thine eyes, nor slumber to thine eyelids (Prov. 6:4).

How long wilt thou sleep, O sluggard? when wilt thou arise out of thy sleep? Yet a little sleep, a little slumber, a little folding of the hands to sleep (Prov. 6:9, 10).

For the drunkard and the glutton shall come to poverty: and drowsiness shall clothe a man with rags (Prov. 23:21).

GOD'S PROMISE FOR TODAY

It is vain for you to rise up early, to sit up late, to eat the bread of sorrows: for so He giveth His beloved sleep (Ps. 127:2).

"Worry comes by human interference with the divine plan."

November

NOVEMBER 1

He that gathereth in summer is a wise son: but he that sleepeth in harvest is a son that causeth shame (Prov. 10:5).

Bring ye all the tithes into the storehouse, that there may be meat in Mine house, and prove Me now herewith, saith the Lord of hosts, if I will not open you the windows of heaven and pour you out a blessing, that there shall not be room enough to receive it (Mal. 3:10).

Behold, the hire of the labourers who have reaped down your fields, which is of you kept back by fraud, crieth: and the cries of them which have reaped are entered into the ears of the Lord of sabaoth (James 5:4).

Then I looked on all the works that my hands had wrought, and on the labour that I had laboured to do: and, behold, all was vanity and vexation of spirit, and there was no profit under the sun (Eccles. 2:11).

GOD'S PROMISE FOR TODAY

He that believeth on the Son hath everlasting life: and he that believeth not the Son shall not see life; but the wrath of God abideth on him (John 3:36).

"I live to die, I die to live; the more I die the more I live."

NOVEMBER 2

His watchmen are blind: they are all ignorant, they are all dumb dogs, they cannot bark; sleeping, lying down, loving to slumber (Isa. 56:10).

Watch ye therefore . . . lest coming suddenly He find you sleeping (Mark 13:35, 36).

According as it written, God hath given them the spirit of slumber, eyes that they should not see, and ears that they should not hear; unto this day (Rom. 11:8).

Therefore let us not sleep, as do others; but let us watch and be sober (I Thess. 5:6).

Love not sleep, lest thou come to poverty: open thine eyes, and thou shalt be satisfied with bread (Prov. 20:13).

GOD'S PROMISE FOR TODAY

And that, knowing the time, that now it is high time to awake out of sleep: for now is our salvation nearer than when we believed (Rom. 13:11).

"Let us be less concerned with what men think we are than with what God knows we are."

NOVEMBER 3

And the second is like, namely this, Thou shalt love thy neighbor as thyself. There is none other commandment greater than these (Mark 12:31).

Love worketh no ill to his neighbour: therefore love is the fulfilling of the law (Rom. 13:10).

We then that are strong ought to bear the infirmities of the weak, and not to please ourselves. Let every one of us please his neighbour for his good to edification (Rom. 15:1, 2).

If ye fulfil the royal law according to the Scripture, Thou shalt love thy neighbour as thyself, ye do well (James 2:8).

For I know your readiness, of which I glory on your behalf to them of Macedonia, that Achaia hath been prepared for a year past; and your zeal hath stirred up very many of them (II Cor. 9:2, RV).

GOD'S PROMISE FOR TODAY

For all the law is fulfilled in one word, even in this; Thou shalt love thy neighbour as thyself (Gal. 5:14).

"Nothing with God can be accidental."

NOVEMBER 4

If thou meet thine enemy's ox or his ass going astray, thou shalt surely bring it back to him again (Exod. 23:4).

If thou see the ass of him that hateth thee lying under his

burden, and wouldest forbear to help him, thou shalt surely help with him (Exod. 23:5).

Rejoice not when thine enemy falleth, and let not thine heart be glad when he stumbleth (Prov. 24:17).

If thine enemy be hungry, give him bread to eat; and if he be thirsty, give him water to drink; for thou shalt heap coals of fire upon his head, and the Lord shall reward thee (Prov. 25:21, 22).

Therefore if thine enemy hunger, feed him; if he thirst, give him drink: for in so doing thou shalt heap coals of fire on his head (Rom. 12:20).

GOD'S PROMISE FOR TODAY

But I say unto you, Love your enemies, bless them that curse you, do good to them that hate you, and pray for them which despitefully use you, and persecute you (Matt. 5:44).

"Attachment to Christ is the only secret of detachment from the world."

NOVEMBER 5

Distributing to the necessity of saints: given to hospitality (Rom. 12:13).

A bishop then must be blameless, the husband of one wife, vigilant, sober, of good behaviour, given to hospitality, apt to teach (I Tim. 3:2).

Well reported of for good works; if she have brought up children, if she have lodged strangers, if she have washed the saints' feet, if she have relieved the afflicted, if she have diligently followed every good work (I Tim. 5:10).

But a lover of hospitality, a lover of good men, sober, just, holy, temperate (Titus 1:8).

Be not forgetful to entertain strangers: for thereby some have entertained angels unawares (Heb. 13:2).

Surely every man walketh in a vain show: surely they are disquieted in vain: he heapeth up riches, and knoweth not who shall gather them (Ps. 39:6).

GOD'S PROMISE FOR TODAY

Use hospitality one to another without grudging (I Peter 4:9).

"It is better to light a candle than to curse the darkness."

They that sow in tears shall reap in joy. He that goeth forth and weepeth, bearing precious seed, shall doubtless come again with rejoicing, bringing his sheaves with him (Ps. 126:5, 6).

Blessed are ye that sow beside all waters, that send forth thither the feet of the ox and the ass (Isa. 32:20).

Sow to yourselves in righteousness, reap in mercy; break up your fallow ground: for it is time to seek the Lord, till He come and rain righteousness upon you (Hos. 10:12).

A sower went out to sow his seed: and as he sowed, some fell by the way side; and it was trodden down, and the fowls of the air devoured it (Luke 8:5).

GOD'S PROMISE FOR TODAY

For he that soweth to his flesh shall of the flesh reap corruption; but he that soweth to the Spirit shall of the Spirit reap life everlasting (Gal. 6:8).

"Yesterday is a canceled check; tomorrow is a promissory note; today is the only cash you have. Spend it wisely."

Then saith He unto His disciples, The harvest truly is plenteous, but the labourers are few (Matt. 9:37).

But when the fruit is brought forth, immediately he putteth in the sickle, because the harvest is come (Mark 4:29).

Therefore said He unto them, The harvest truly is great, but the labourers are few: pray ye therefore the Lord of the harvest, that He would send forth labourers into His harvest (Luke 10:2).

Say not ye, There are yet four months, and then cometh harvest? behold, I say unto you, Lift up your eyes and look on the fields; for they are white already to harvest. And he that reapeth receiveth wages, and gathered fruit unto life eternal: that both he that soweth and he that reapeth may rejoice together (John 4:35, 36).

GOD'S PROMISE FOR TODAY

And let us not be weary in well doing: for in due season we shall reap, if we faint not (Gal. 6:9).

"It is not how much we have but how much we enjoy that makes happiness."

NOVEMBER 8

Stand fast therefore in the liberty wherewith Christ hath made us free, and be not entangled again with the yoke of bondage (Gal. 5:1).

Only let your conversation be as it becometh the gospel of Christ: that whether I come and see you, or else be absent I may hear of your affairs, that ye stand fast in one spirit, with one mind striving together for the faith of the gospel (Phil. 1:27).

Whom resist stedfast in the faith, knowing that the same afflictions are accomplished in your brethren that are in the world (I Peter 5:9).

Ye therefore, beloved, seeing ye know these things before, beware lest ye also being led away with the error of the wicked, fall from our own stedfastness (II Peter 3:17).

GOD'S PROMISE FOR TODAY

Therefore, my beloved brethren, be ye stedfast, unmoveable, always abounding in the work of the Lord, forasmuch as ye know that your labour is not in vain in the Lord (I Cor. 15:58).

"Are you enjoying your trip through life or are you worrying about your baggage?"

NOVEMBER 9

And ye shall be hated of all men for My name's sake: but he that endureth to the end shall be saved (Matt. 10:22).

If ye endure chastening, God dealeth with you as with sons; for what son is he whom the father chasteneth not? (Heb. 12:7).

Behold, we count them happy which endure. Ye have heard of the patience of Job, and have seen the end of the Lord: that the Lord is very pitiful, and of tender mercy (James 5:11).

For this is thankworthy, if a man for conscience toward God endure grief, suffering wrongfully (I Peter 2:19).

And it came to pass in those days, that He went out into a mountain to pray, and continued all night in prayer to God (Luke 6:12).

GOD'S PROMISE FOR TODAY

Blessed is the man that endureth temptation: for when he is tried, he shall receive the crown of life, which the Lord hath promised to them that love Him (James 1:12).

"A puppy plays with every pup he meets, but an old dog has few associates."

As the Father hath loved Me, so have I loved you: continue ye in My love (John 15:9).

And let us not be weary in well doing: for in due season we shall reap, if we faint not (Gal. 6:9).

Wherefore, seeing we also are compassed about with so great a cloud of witnesses, let us lay aside every weight, and the sin which doth so easily beset us, and let us run with patience the race that is set before us (Heb. 12:1).

Wherefore gird up the loins of your mind, be sober, and hope to the end for grace that is to be brought unto you at the revelation of Jesus Christ (I Peter 1:13).

Behold, I come quickly: hold that fast which thou hast, that no man take thy crown (Rev. 3:11).

GOD'S PROMISE FOR TODAY

The righteous also shall hold on his way, and he that hath clean hands shall be stronger and stronger (Job 17:9).

" 'Tis not the hen that cackles most that lays the most eggs."

My son, fear thou the Lord and the king: and meddle not with them that are given to change (Prov. 24:21).

Why gaddest thou about so much to change thy way? thou also shalt be ashamed of Egypt, as thou wast ashamed of Assyria (Jer. 2:36).

That we henceforth be no more children, tossed to and fro, and carried about with every wind of doctrine by the sleight of men, and cunning craftiness, whereby they lie in wait to deceive (Eph. 4:14).

Be not carried about with divers and strange doctrines; for it is a good thing that the heart be established with grace; not with meats, which have not profited them that have been occupied therein (Heb. 13:9).

GOD'S PROMISE FOR TODAY

But let him ask in faith, nothing wavering: for he that wavereth is like a wave of the sea driven with the wind and tossed (James 1:6).

"You can't hitchhike on the road to heaven."

But I say unto you, That every idle word that men shall speak, they shall give account thereof in the day of judgment (Matt. 12:36).

But God said unto him, Thou fool, this night thy soul shall be required of thee: then whose shall those things be, which thou hast provided? (Luke 12:20).

But he that knew not, and did commit things worthy of stripes, shall be beaten with few stripes. For unto whomsoever much is given, of him shall be much required; and to whom men have committed much, of him they will ask the more (Luke 12:48).

And it came to pass, that when he was returned, having received the kingdom, then he commanded these servants to be called unto thim, to whom he had given the money, that he might know how much every man had gained by trading (Luke 19:15).

GOD'S PROMISE FOR TODAY

So then every one of us shall give account of himself to God (Rom. 14:12).

"It costs nothing *to become* a Christian, but it costs every-things *to be* a Christian."

And they departed from the presence of the council, rejoicing that they were counted worthy to suffer shame for His name (Acts 5:41).

And if children, then heirs; heirs of God, and joint heirs with Christ; if so be that we suffer with Him, that we may be also glorified together (Rom. 8:17).

Take, my brethren, the prophets, who have spoken in the name of the Lord, for an example of suffering, affliction, and of patience (James 5:10).

For what glory is it, if, when ye be buffeted for your faults, ye shall take it patiently? but if, when ye do well, and suffer for it, ye take it patiently, this is acceptable with God (I Peter 2:20).

But the God of all grace, Who hath called us unto His eternal glory by Christ Jesus, after that ye have suffered a while, make you perfect, stablish, strengthen, settle you (I Peter 5:10).

Choosing rather to suffer affliction with the people of God, than to enjoy the pleasures of sin for a season (Heb. 11:25).

"Opportunity for distinction lies in doing ordinary things extra-ordinarily well."

NOVEMBER 14

And ye shall be hated of all men for My name's sake: but he that endureth to the end shall be saved (Matt. 10:22).

He that findeth his life shall lose it: and he that loseth his life for My sake shall find it (Matt. 10:39).

And every one that hath forsaken houses, or brethren, or sisters, or father, or mother, or wife, or children, or land, for My name's sake, shall receive a hundredfold, and shall inherit everlasting life (Matt. 19:29).

We are fools for Christ's sake, but ye are wise in Christ: we are weak, but ye are strong; ye are honourable, but we are despised (I Cor. 4:10).

For we which live are always delivered unto death for Jesus' sake, that the life also of Jesus might be made manifest in our mortal flesh (II Cor. 4:11).

GOD'S PROMISE FOR TODAY

Blessed are ye, when men shall revile you, and persecute you, and shall say all manner of evil against you falsely, for My sake (Matt. 5:11).

"The worst wheel on the cart makes the most noise."

NOVEMBER 15

I gave my back to the smiters, and My cheeks to them that plucked off the hair: I hid not My face from shame and spitting (Isa. 50:6).

For it became Him, for Whom are all things, and by Whom are all things, in bringing many sons unto glory, to make the captain of their salvation perfect through sufferings (Heb. 2:10).

Wherefore Jesus also, that He might sanctify the people with His own blood, suffered without the gate (Heb. 13:12).

For Christ also hath once suffered for sins, the just for the unjust, that He might bring us to God, being put to death in the flesh, but quickened by the Spirit (I Peter 3:18).

But He was wounded for our transgressions, He was bruised for our iniquities: the chastisement of our peace was upon Him; and with His stripes we are healed (Isa. 53:5).

"He that's content hath enough. He that complains has too much."

NOVEMBER 16

God forbid. How shall we, that are dead to sin, live any longer therein? (Rom. 6:2).

Likewise reckon ye also yourselves to be dead indeed unto sin, but alive unto God through Jesus Christ our Lord (Rom. 6:11).

And they that are Christ's have crucified the flesh with the affections and lusts (Gal. 5:24).

For ye are dead, and your life is hid with Christ in God (Col. 3:3).

Who His own self bare our sins in His own body on the tree, that we, being dead to sins, should live unto righteousness: by Whose stripes ye were healed (I Peter 2:24).

GOD'S PROMISE FOR TODAY

But God forbid that I should glory, save in the cross of our Lord Jesus Christ, by Whom the world is crucified unto me, and I unto the world (Gal. 6:14).

"Sin may come upon thee by surprise, but do not let it dwell with thee as a guest."

NOVEMBER 17

What! know ye not that your body is the temple of the Holy Ghost which is in you, which ye have of God, and ye are not your own? (I Cor. 6:19).

And what agreement hath the temple of God with idols? for ye are the temple of the living God; as God hath said, I will dwell in them, and walk in them; and I will be their God, and they shall be My people (II Cor. 6:16).

And are built upon the foundation of the apostles and prophets, Jesus Christ Himself being the chief corner stone; in Whom all the building fitly framed together groweth unto a holy temple in the Lord; in Whom ye also are builded together for a habitation of God through the Spirit (Eph. 2:20-22).

Ye also, as lively stones, are built up a spiritual house, a holy priesthood, to offer up spiritual sacrifices, acceptable to God by Jesus Christ (I Peter 2:5).

GOD'S PROMISE FOR TODAY

Know ye not that ye are the temple of God, and that the Spirit of God dwelleth in you? (I Cor. 3:16).

"Where one goes *hereafter* depends largely upon what he goes *after here*."

NOVEMBER 18

At that day ye shall know that I am in My Father, and ye in Me, and I in you (John 14:20).

I in them, and Thou in me, that they may be made perfect in one; and that the world may know that Thou hast sent Me, and hast loved them, as Thou hast loved Me (John 17:23).

I am crucified with Christ; nevertheless I live; yet not I, but Christ liveth in me: and the life which I now live in the flesh I live by the faith of the Son of God, Who loved me, and gave Himself for me (Gal. 2:20).

To Whom God would make known what is the riches of the glory of this mystery among the Gentiles; which is Christ in you, the hope of glory (Col. 1:27).

GOD'S PROMISE FOR TODAY

Behold, I stand at the door, and knock: if any man hear my voice, and open the door, I will come in to him, and will sup with him, and he with Me (Rev. 3:20).

"Habit is a cable; we weave a thread of it each day until at last we cannot break it."

NOVEMBER 19

There hath no temptation taken you but such as is common to man: but God is faithful, Who will not suffer you to be tempted above that ye are able; but will with the temptation also make a way of escape, that ye may be able to bear it (I Cor. 10:13).

My brethren, count it all joy when ye fall into divers temptations; knowing this, that the trying of your faith worketh patience (James 1:2, 3).

Blessed is the man that endureth temptation: for when he is tried, he shall receive the crown of life, which the Lord hath promised to them that love Him (James 1:12).

Because thou hast kept the word of My patience, I also will keep thee from the hour of temptation, which shall come upon all the world, to try them that dwell upon the earth (Rev. 3:10).

GOD'S PROMISE FOR TODAY

The Lord knoweth how to deliver the godly out of temptations, and to reserve the unjust unto the day of judgment to be punished (II Peter 2:9).

"Don't spend your health to gain wealth, then spend your wealth to regain health."

NOVEMBER 20

Ye are My witnesses, saith the Lord, and My servant whom I have chosen; that ye may know and believe Me, and understand that I am He: before Me there was no God formed, neither shall there be after Me (Isa. 43:10).

And ye also shall bear witness, because ye have been with Me from the beginning (John 15:27).

Then spake the Lord to Paul in the night by a vision, Be not afraid, but speak, and hold not thy peace: for I am with thee, and no man shall set on thee to hurt thee: for I have much people in this city (Acts 18:9, 10).

And he said, The God of our fathers hath chosen thee, that thou shouldest know His will, and see that Just One, and shouldest hear the voice of His mouth. For thou shalt be His witness unto all men of what thou hast seen and heard (Acts 22:14, 15).

GOD'S PROMISE FOR TODAY

These things speak, and exhort, and rebuke with all authority. Let no man despise thee (Titus 2:15).

"Fear not tomorrow. God is already there."

NOVEMBER 21

So we, being many, are one body in Christ, and every one members one of another (Rom. 12:5).

For we being many are one bread, and one body: for we are all partakers of that one bread (I Cor. 10:17).

There is neither Jew nor Greek, there is neither bond nor free, there is neither male nor female: for ye are all one in Christ Jesus (Gal. 3:28).

Till we all come in the unity of the faith, and of the knowledge of the Son of God, unto a perfect man, unto the measure of stature of the fulness of Christ (Eph. 4:13).

Go, stand and speak in the temple to the people all the words of this life. And when they heard that, they entered into the temple early in the morning and taught (Acts 5:20, 21).

GOD'S PROMISE FOR TODAY

Where there is neither Greek nor Jew, circumcision nor uncircumcision, Barbarian, Scythian, bond nor free: but Christ is all, and in all (Col. 3:11).

"It's what you learn after you know it all that counts."

NOVEMBER 22

Now I beseech you, brethren, by the name of our Lord Jesus Christ, that ye all speak the same thing, and that there be no divisions among you; but that ye be perfectly joined together in the same mind and in the same judgment (I Cor. 1:10).

Finally, brethren, farewell. Be perfect, be of good comfort, be of one mind, live in peace; and the God of love and peace shall be with you (II Cor. 13:11).

Endeavoring to keep the unity of the Spirit in the bond of peace (Eph. 4:3).

Only let your conversation be as it becometh the gospel of Christ: that whether I come and see you, or else be absent, I may hear of your affairs, that ye stand fast in one spirit, with one mind striving together for the faith of the gospel (Phil. 1:27).

GOD'S PROMISE FOR TODAY

Finally, be ye all of one mind, having compassion one of another; love as brethren, be pitiful, be courteous (I Peter 3:8).

"A good conscience is a soft pillow."

NOVEMBER 23

Strive not with a man without cause, if he have done thee no harm (Prov. 3:30).

The beginning of strife is as when one letteth out water: therefore leave off contention, before it be meddled with (Prov. 17:14).

Go not forth hastily to strive, lest thou know not what to do in the end thereof, when thy neighbour hath put thee to shame (Prov. 25:8).

He that passeth by, and meddleth with strife belonging not to him, is like one that taketh a dog by the ears (Prov. 26:17).

Of these things put them in remembrance, charging them before the Lord that they strive not about words to no profit, but to the subverting of the hearers (II Tim. 2:14).

And the servant of the Lord must not strive; but be gentle unto all men, apt to teach, patient (II Tim. 2:24).

GOD'S PROMISE FOR TODAY

It is an honour for a man to cease from strife: but every fool will be meddling (Prov. 20:3).

"Giving is true having."

NOVEMBER 24

Therefore we are buried with Him by baptism into death: that like as Christ was raised up from the dead by the glory of the Father, even so we also should walk in newness of life (Rom. 6:4).

This I say then, walk in the Spirit, and ye shall not fulfil the lust of the flesh (Gal. 5:16).

And walk in love, as Christ also hath loved us, and hath given Himself for us an offering and a sacrifice to God for a sweet-smelling savour (Eph. 5:2).

See then that ye walk circumspectly, not as fools, but as wise (Eph. 5:15).

He that saith he abideth in Him ought himself also so to walk, even as He walketh (I John 2:6).

GOD'S PROMISE FOR TODAY

But if we walk in the light, as He is in the light, we have fellowship one with another, and the blood of Jesus Christ His Son cleanseth us from all sin (I John 1:7).

"When God denies His child anything, it is with the design to give him something better."

NOVEMBER 25

Watch and pray, that ye enter not into temptation: the spirit indeed is willing, but the flesh is weak (Matt. 26:41).

Therefore watch, and remember, that by the space of three years I ceased not to warn every one night and day with tears (Acts 20:31).

Wherefore let him that thinketh he standeth take heed lest he fall (I Cor. 10:12).

Watch ye, stand fast in the faith, quit you like men, be strong (I Cor. 16:13).

Continue in prayer, and watch in the same with thanksgiving (Col. 4:2).

I therefore, the prisoner of the Lord, beseech you that ye walk worthy of the vocation wherewith ye are called (Eph. 4:1).

GOD'S PROMISE FOR TODAY

Be sober, be vigilant; because your adversary the devil, as a roaring lion, walketh about, seeking whom he may devour (I Peter 5:8).

"Why worry when you can pray?"

NOVEMBER 26

Out of the mouth of babes and sucklings hast Thou ordained strength because of Thine enemies, that Thou mightest still the enemy and the avenger (Ps. 8:2).

But God hath chosen the foolish things of the world to confound the wise; and God hath chosen the weak things of the world to confound the things which are mighty (I Cor. 1:27).

Who through faith subdued kingdoms, wrought righteousness, obtained promises, stopped the mouths of lions, quenched the violence of fire, escaped the edge of the sword, out of weakness were made strong, waxed valiant in fight, turned to flight the armies of the aliens (Heb. 11:33, 34).

GOD'S PROMISE FOR TODAY

And He said unto me, My grace is sufficient for thee; for My strength is made perfect in weakness. Most gladly therefore will I rather glory in my infirmities, that the power of Christ rest upon me (II Cor. 12:9).

"No tent is so good to live in as content."

NOVEMBER 27

Ye shall not afflict any widow, or fatherless child (Exod. 22:22).

Thou shalt not pervert the judgment of the stranger, nor of the fatherless; nor take a widow's raiment to pledge (Deut. 24:17).

When thou hast made an end of tithing all the tithes of thine increase the third year, which is the year of tithing, and hast given it unto the Levite, the stranger, the fatherless, and the widow, that they may eat within thy gates, and be filled (Deut. 26:12).

Remove not the old landmark; and enter not into the fields of the fatherless (Prov. 23:10).

Pure religion and undefiled before God and the Father is this, To visit the fatherless and widows in their affliction, and to keep himself unspotted from the world (James 1:27).

GOD'S PROMISE FOR TODAY

Learn to do well; seek judgment, relieve the oppressed, judge the fatherless, plead for the widow (Isa. 1:17).

"Do you throw shadows or sunbeams?"

NOVEMBER 28

Verily, verily, I say unto you, if a man keep My saying, he shall never see death (John 8:51).

If ye love Me, keep My commandments. And I will pray the Father and He shall give you another Comforter, that He may abide with you for ever (John 14:15, 16).

Jesus answered and said unto him, If a man love Me, he will keep My words: and My Father will love him and We will come unto him, and make our abode with him (John 14:23).

I have manifested Thy name unto the men which Thou gavest Me out of the world: Thine they were, and Thou gavest them Me; and they have kept Thy word (John 17:6).

I know thy works: behold, I have set before thee an open door, and no man can shut it: for thou hast a little strength, and hast kept My word, and hast not denied My name (Rev. 3:8).

GOD'S PROMISE FOR TODAY

And hereby we do know that we know Him, if we keep His commandments (I John 2:3).

"No wind can do him any good who steers for no port."

NOVEMBER 29

That they do good, that they be rich in good works, ready to distribute, willing to communicate (I Tim. 6:18).

In all things shewing thyself a pattern of good works: in doctrine shewing uncorruptness, gravity, sincerity (Titus 2:7).

And let us consider one another to provoke unto love and to good works (Heb. 10:24).

Even so faith, if it hath not works, is dead, being alone. Yea, a man may say, thou hast faith, and I have works: shew me thy faith without thy works, and I will shew thee my faith by my works (James 2:17, 18).

Having your conversation honest among the Gentiles: that, whereas they speak against you as evil doers, they may by your good works, which they shall behold, glorify God in the day of visitation (I Peter 2:12).

GOD'S PROMISE FOR TODAY

Let your light so shine before men, that they may see your good works, and glorify your Father which is in heaven (Matt. 5:16).

"God always gives His best to those who leave the choice with Him."

NOVEMBER 30

Many will say to Me in that day, Lord, Lord, have we not prophesied in Thy name? and in Thy name have cast out devils? and in Thy name done many wonderful works? And then will I profess unto them, I never knew you: depart from Me, ye that work iniquity (Matt. 7:22, 23).

Knowing that a man is not justified by the works of the law, but by the faith of Jesus Christ, even we have believed in Jesus Christ, that we might be justified by the faith of Christ, and not by the works of the law: for by the works of the law shall no flesh be justified (Gal. 2:16).

Not by works of righteousness which we have done, but according to His mercy He saved us, by the washing of regeneration, and renewing of the Holy Ghost (Titus 3:5).

GOD'S PROMISE FOR TODAY

For by grace are ye saved through faith; and that not of yourselves: it is the gift of God. Not of works, lest any man should boast (Eph. 2:8, 9).

"The way to avoid great faults is to beware of small ones."

December

DECEMBER 1

Depart from evil, and do good; seek peace, and pursue it (Ps. 34:14).

But love ye your enemies and do good, and lend, hoping for nothing again; and your reward shall be great, and ye shall be the children of the Highest: for He is kind unto the unthankful and to the evil (Luke 6:35).

But to do good and to communicate forget not: for with such sacrifices God is well pleased (Heb. 13:16).

Therefore to him that knoweth to do good, and doeth it not, to him it is sin (James 4:17).

Therefore I take pleasure in infirmities, in reproaches, in necessities, in persecutions, in distresses for Christ's sake; for when I am weak, then am I strong (II Cor. 12:10).

GOD'S PROMISE FOR TODAY

Trust in the Lord, and do good; so shalt thou dwell in the land, and verily thou shalt be fed (Ps. 37:3).

"Wisdom is knowing when to speak your mind and when to mind your speech."

DECEMBER 2

And they that be wise shall shine as the brightness of the firmament and they that turn many to righteousness, as the stars for ever and ever (Dan. 12:3).

And He saith unto them, Follow Me, and I will make you fishers of men (Matt. 4:19).

For though I be free from all men, yet have I made myself servant unto all, that I might gain the more. And unto the Jews I became as a Jew, that I might gain the Jews; to them that are under the law (I Cor. 9:19, 20).

And others save with fear, pulling them out of the fire; hating even the garment spotted by the flesh (Jude 23).

Therefore by the deeds of the law there shall no flesh be justified in His sight: for by the law is the knowledge of sin (Rom. 3:20).

GOD'S PROMISE FOR TODAY

The fruit of the righteous is a tree of life; and he that winneth souls is wise (Prov. 11:30).

"The best way to get rid of unpleasant duties is to discharge them faithfully."

DECEMBER 3

For what is a man profited, if he shall gain the whole world, and lose his own soul, or what shall a man give in exchange for his soul? (Matt. 16:26).

And take heed to yourselves, lest at any time your hearts be overcharged with surfeiting, and drunkenness, and cares of this life, and so that day come upon you unawares (Luke 21:34).

Set your affection on things above, not on things on the earth (Col. 3:2).

Teaching us that, denying ungodliness and worldly lusts, we should live soberly, righteously, and godly, in this present world (Titus 2:12).

Let nothing be done through strife or vainglory; but in lowliness of mind let each esteem other better than themselves (Phil. 2:3).

GOD'S PROMISE FOR TODAY

Ye adulterers and adulteresses, know ye not that the friendship of the world is enmity with God? Whosoever therefore will be a friend of the world is the enemy of God (James 4:4).

"People may forget how *fast* you did a job, but they will remember how *well* you did it."

DECEMBER 4

And be not conformed to this world: but be ye transformed

by the renewing of your mind, that ye may prove what is that good and acceptable, and perfect will of God (Rom. 12:2).

But God forbid that I should glory, save in the cross of our Lord Jesus Christ, by Whom the world is crucified unto me, and I unto the world (Gal. 6:14).

No man that warreth entangleth himself with the affairs of this life; that he may please Him Who hath chosen him to be a soldier (II Tim. 2:4).

By faith Moses, when he was come to years, refused to be called the son of Pharaoh's daughter; choosing rather to suffer affliction with the people of God, than to enjoy the pleasures of sin for a season (Heb. 11:24, 25).

GOD'S PROMISE FOR TODAY

Love not the world, neither the things that are in the world. If any man love the world, the love of the Father is not in him (I John 2:15).

"If we would own a part of God's all, we must disown all apart from God."

DECEMBER 5

Moreover, because I have set my affection to the house of my God, I have of mine own proper good, of gold and silver, which I have given to the house of my God, over and above all that I have prepared for the holy house (I Chron. 29:3).

Surely goodness and mercy shall follow me all the days of my life: and I will dwell in the house of the Lord forever (Ps. 23:6).

One thing have I desired of the Lord, that will I seek after; that I may dwell in the house of the Lord all the days of my life, to behold the beauty of the Lord, and to enquire in His temple (Ps. 27:4).

I was glad when they said unto me, let us go into the house of the Lord (Ps. 122:1).

GOD'S PROMISE FOR TODAY

For a day in Thy courts is better than a thousand. I had rather be a doorkeeper in the house of my God, than to dwell in the tents of wickedness (Ps. 84:10).

"It is wrong for a person to profess what he does not possess."

DECEMBER 6

Cease from anger, and forsake wrath: fret not thyself in any wise to do evil (Ps. 37:8).

He that is soon angry dealeth foolishly: and a man of wicked devices is hated (Prov. 14:17).

The discretion of a man deferreth his anger; and it is his glory to pass over a transgression (Prov. 19:11).

Be not hasty in thy spirit to be angry: for anger resteth in the bosom of fools (Eccles. 7:9).

But I say unto you, That whosoever is angry with his brother without a cause shall be in danger of the judgment: and whosoever shall say to his brother, Raca, shall be in danger of the council: but whosoever shall say, Thou fool, shall be in danger of hell fire (Matt. 5:22).

Wherefore, my beloved brethren, let every man be swift to hear, slow to speak, slow to wrath (James 1:19).

GOD'S PROMISE FOR TODAY

He that is slow to anger is better than the mighty; and he that ruleth his spirit than he that taketh a city (Prov. 16:32).

"In order to mold His people, God often has to melt them."

DECEMBER 7

Wherewithal shall a young man cleanse his way? by taking heed thereto according to Thy word (Ps. 119:9).

Rejoice, O young man, in thy youth; and let thy heart cheer thee in the days of thy youth, and walk in the ways of thine heart, and in the sight of thine eyes: but know thou, that for all these things God will bring thee unto judgment (Eccles. 11:9).

Young men likewise exhort to be soberminded. In all things shewing thyself a pattern of good works: in doctrine shewing uncorruptness, gravity, sincerity (Titus 2:6, 7).

The glory of young men is their strength (Prov. 20:29).

I write unto you, young men, because ye have overcome the wicked one. I write unto you, little children, because ye have known the Father. I have written unto you, young men because ye are strong, and the word of God abideth in you (I John 2:13, 14).

GOD'S PROMISE FOR TODAY

It is good for a man that he bear the yoke in his youth (Lam. 3:27).

"To escape criticism, do nothing, say nothing, be nothing."

DECEMBER 8

For it is not ye that speak, but the Spirit of your Father which speaketh in you (Matt. 10:20).

But when they shall lead you, and deliver you up, take no thought beforehand what ye shall speak, neither do ye premeditate: but whatsoever shall be given you in that hour, that speak ye: for it is not ye that speak, but the Holy Ghost (Mark 13:11).

Which things also we speak, not in the words which man's wisdom teacheth, but which the Holy Ghost teacheth; comparing spiritual things with spiritual (I Cor. 2:13).

If any man speak, let him speak as the oracles of God (I Peter 4:11).

For the prophecy came not in old time by the will of man: but holy men of God spake as they were moved by the Holy Ghost (II Peter 1:21).

GOD'S PROMISE FOR TODAY

He that believeth on Me, as the scripture hath said, from within him shall flow rivers of living water (John 7:38, RV).

"Of greater importance is not the *out*fit but rather the *in*fit."

DECEMBER 9

Then said Jesus unto them again, Verily, verily, I say unto you, I am the door of the sheep (John 10:7).

By Whom also we have access by faith into this grace wherein we stand, and rejoice in hope of the glory of God (Rom. 5:2).

For through Him we both have access by one Spirit unto the Father (Eph. 2:18).

The Holy Ghost this signifying, that the way into the holiest of all was not yet made manifest, while as the first tabernacle was yet standing (Heb. 9:8).

Having therefore, brethren, boldness to enter into the holiest by the blood of Jesus, by a new and living way, which He hath consecrated for us, through the veil, that is to say, His flesh (Heb. 10:19, 20).

GOD'S PROMISE FOR TODAY

Jesus saith unto him, I am the way, the truth, and the life: no man cometh unto the Father, but by Me (John 14:6).

"A knocker never wins, and a winner never knocks."

DECEMBER 10

Bring forth therefore fruits meet for repentance (Matt. 3:8).

Let your light so shine before men, that they may see your good works, and glorify your Father which is in heaven (Matt. 5:16).

And these are they which are sown on good ground; such as hear the word, and receive it, and bring forth fruit, some thirty-fold, some sixty, and some an hundred (Mark 4:20).

And if it bear fruit, well: and if not, then after that thou shalt cut it down (Luke 13:9).

Ye have not chosen Me, but I have chosen you, and ordained you, that ye should go and bring forth fruit, and that your fruit should remain: that whatsoever ye shall ask of the Father in My name, He may give it to you (John 15:16).

GOD'S PROMISE FOR TODAY

Herein is My Father glorified, that ye bear much fruit; so shall ye be My disciples (John 15:8).

"Providence sends food to the birds, but does not throw it into the nest."

DECEMBER 11

The mouth of the just bringeth forth wisdom: but the froward tongue shall be cut out (Prov. 10:31).

And if thy right hand offend thee, cut it off, and cast it from thee: for it is profitable for thee that one of thy members should perish, and not that thy whole body should be cast into hell (Matt. 5:30).

In Whom also ye are circumcised with the circumcision made without hands, in putting off the body of the sins of the flesh by the circumcision of Christ (Col. 2:11).

Mortify therefore your members which are upon the earth; fornication, uncleanness, inordinate affection, evil concupiscence, and covetousness, which is idolatry (Col. 3:5).

GOD'S PROMISE FOR TODAY

For if ye live after the flesh, ye shall die; but if ye through the Spirit do mortify the deeds of the body, ye shall live (Rom. 8:13).

"If trouble drives you to pray, prayer will drive the trouble away."

DECEMBER 12

Jesus said unto him, if thou wilt be perfect, go and sell that thou hast, and give to the poor, and thou shalt have treasure in heaven: and come and follow Me (Matt. 19:21).

And every one that hath forsaken houses, or brethren, or sisters, or father, or mother, or wife, or children, or lands, for My name's sake, shall receive an hundredfold, and shall inherit everlasting life (Matt. 19:29).

And He sat down, and called the twelve, and saith unto them, If any man desire to be first, the same shall be last of all, and servant of all (Mark 9:35).

Yea doubtless, and I count all things but loss for the excellency of the knowledge of Christ Jesus my Lord: for Whom I have suffered the loss of all things, and do count them but dung, that I may win Christ (Phil. 3:8).

GOD'S PROMISE FOR TODAY

Verily, verily, I say unto you, Except a corn of wheat fall into the ground and die, it abideth alone: but if it die, it bringeth forth much fruit (John 12:24).

"When you meet temptation turn to the 'Right.'"

DECEMBER 13

Teaching them to observe all things whatsoever I have commanded you; and, lo, I am with you alway, even unto the end of the world. Amen (Matt. 28:20).

Abide in Me, and I in you. As the branch cannot bear fruit of itself, except it abide in the vine; no more can ye, except ye abide in Me (John 15:4).

I in them, and Thou in Me, that they may be made perfect in one; and that the world may know that Thou hast sent me, and hast loved them, as Thou hast loved Me (John 17:23).

For I am persuaded, that neither death, nor life, nor angels, nor principalities, nor powers, nor things present, nor things to come, nor height, nor depth, nor any other creature, shall be able to separate us from the love of God, which is in Christ Jesus our Lord (Rom. 8:38, 39).

GOD'S PROMISE FOR TODAY

And I give unto them eternal life; and they shall never perish, neither shall any man pluck them out of My hand (John 10:28).

"Character is the poor man's saving bank."

DECEMBER 14

By this shall all men know that ye are My disciples, if ye have love one to another (John 13:35).

He saith to him again the second time, Simon, son of Jonas, lovest thou Me? He saith unto Him, yea, Lord; Thou knowest that I love Thee. He saith unto him, Feed My sheep (John 21:16).

We know that we have passed from death unto life, because we love the brethren. He that loveth not his brother abideth in death (I John 3:14).

If a man say, I love God and hateth his brother, he is a liar: for he that loveth not his brother whom he hath seen, how can he love God whom he hath not seen? (I John 4:20).

GOD'S PROMISE FOR TODAY

Though I speak with the tongues of men and of angels, and have not charity, I am become as sounding brass, or a tinkling cymbal (I Cor. 13:1).

"Be like the watch: have an open face and busy hands, be full of good works and pure gold, and be well regulated."

DECEMBER 15

For God so loved the world, that He gave His only begotten Son, that whosoever believeth in Him should not perish, but have everlasting life (John 3:16).

Then Simon Peter answered Him, Lord, to whom shall we go? Thou hast the words of eternal life (John 6:68).

I said therefore unto you, that ye shall die in your sins: for if ye believe not that I am He, ye shall die in your sins (John 8:24).

Neither is there salvation in any other: for there is none other name under heaven given among men, whereby we must be saved (Acts 4:12).

For other foundation can no man lay than that is laid, which is Jesus Christ (I Cor. 3:11).

GOD'S PROMISE FOR TODAY

For I determined not to know any thing among you, save Jesus Christ, and Him crucified (I Cor. 2:2).

"A living Christ in a living man is a living sermon."

DECEMBER 16

And He said unto them, Go ye into all the world, and preach the gospel to every creature (Mark 16:15).

Teaching them to observe all things whatsoever I have commanded you; and lo, I am with you alway, even unto the end of the world (Matt. 28:20).

For every one that asketh receiveth; and he that seeketh findeth; and to Him that knocketh it shall be opened (Luke 11:10).

Then Peter opened his mouth, and said, Of a truth I perceive that God is no respecter of persons (Acts 10:34).

For there is no difference between the Jew and the Greek: for the same Lord over all is rich unto all that call upon Him (Rom. 10:12).

GOD'S PROMISE FOR TODAY

And the Spirit and the bride say, Come. And let him that heareth say, Come. And let him that is athirst come. And whosoever will, let him take the water of life freely (Rev. 22:17).

"Speak kind words and you will hear kind echoes."

DECEMBER 17

And they that be wise shall shine as the brightness of the firmament; and they that turn many to righteousness, as the stars for ever and ever (Dan. 12:3).

For the Son of man shall come in the glory of His Father with his angels; and then He shall reward every man according to his works (Matt. 16:27).

Who shall not receive manifold more in this present time, and in the world to come life everlasting (Luke 18:30).

Now he that planteth and he that watereth are one: and every man shall receive his own reward according to his own labour (I Cor. 3:8).

And, behold, I come quickly; and My reward is with Me, to give every man according as his work shall be (Rev. 22:12).

GOD'S PROMISE FOR TODAY

But this I say, He which soweth sparingly shall reap also sparingly: and he which soweth bountifully shall reap also bountifully (II Cor. 9:6).

"God's part we cannot do; our part He will not do."

DECEMBER 18

For I am persuaded, that neither death, nor life, nor angels nor principalities, nor powers, nor things present, nor things to come, nor height, nor death, nor any other creature, shall be able to separate us from the love of God, which is in Christ Jesus our Lord (Rom. 8:38, 39).

For the which cause I also suffer these things: nevertheless I am not ashamed: for I know Whom I have believed, and am persuaded that He is able to keep that which I have committed unto Him against that day (II Tim. 1:12).

Let no man despise thy youth; but be thou an example of the believers, in word, in conversation, in charity, in spirit, in faith, in purity (I Tim. 4:12).

For in that He Himself hath suffered being tempted, He is able to succour them that are tempted (Heb. 2:18).

GOD'S PROMISE FOR TODAY

And being fully persuaded that, what He had promised, He was able also to perform (Rom. 4:21).

"Don't make up your mind until you know the facts."

DECEMBER 19

For the Lord of hosts hath purposed, and who shall disannul it? and His hand is stretched out, and who shall turn it back? (Isa. 14:27).

But rise, and stand upon thy feet: for I have appeared unto thee for this purpose, to make thee a minister and a witness both of these things which thou hast seen, and of those things in the which I will appear unto thee (Acts 26:16).

Having made known unto us the mystery of His will, according to His good pleasure which He hath purposed in Himself (Eph. 1:9).

He that commiteth sin is of the devil; for the devil sinneth from the beginning. For this purpose the Son of God was manifested, that He might destroy the works of the devil (I John 3:8).

GOD'S PROMISE FOR TODAY

According to the eternal purpose which He purposed in Christ Jesus our Lord (Eph. 3:11).

"The devil has to work hard for all he gets in the home of a praying mother."

DECEMBER 20

Blessed is the man that walketh not in the counsel of the ungodly, nor standeth in the way of sinners, nor sitteth in the seat of the scornful (Ps. 1:1).

And he shall be like a tree planted by the rivers of water, that bringeth forth his fruit in his season; his leaf also shall not wither; and whatsoever he doeth shall prosper. The ungodly are not so: but are like the chaff which the wind driveth away. Therefore the ungodly shall not stand in the judgment, nor sinners in the congregation of the righteous. For the Lord knoweth the way of the righteous: but the way of the ungodly shall perish (Ps. 1:3-6).

Sing unto the Lord a new song, and His praise from the end of the earth, ye that go down to the sea, and all that is therein; the isles, and the inhabitants thereof (Isa. 42:10).

GOD'S PROMISE FOR TODAY

But his delight is in the law of the Lord; and in His law doth he meditate day and night (Ps. 1:2).

"Everything is wrong that is almost right."

DECEMBER 21

I will love Thee, O Lord, my strength (Ps. 18:1).

I will call upon the Lord, Who is worthy to be praised; so shall I be saved from mine enemies. The sorrows of death compassed me, and the floods of ungodly men made me afraid. The sorrows of hell compassed me about: the snares of death prevented me. In my distress I called upon the Lord, and cried unto my God: He heard my voice out of His temple, and my cry came before Him, even into His ears (Ps. 18:3-6).

Lord, I have loved the habitation of Thy house, and the place where thine honor dwelleth (Ps. 26:8).

For I will shew him how great things he must suffer for My name's sake (Acts 9:16).

GOD'S PROMISE FOR TODAY

The Lord is my rock, and my fortress, and my deliverer; my God, my strength, in Whom I will trust; my buckler, and the horn of my salvation, and my high tower (Ps. 18:2).

"You tell how near one lives to God, if you know how far he lives from sin."

DECEMBER 22

The Lord is my shepherd: I shall not want. He maketh me to lie down in green pastures: He leadeth me beside the still waters. He restoreth my soul: He leadeth me in the paths of righteousness for His name's sake (Ps. 23:1-3).

Thou preparest a table before me in the presence of mine enemies: Thou anointest my head with oil; my cup runneth over. Surely goodness and mercy shall follow me all the days of my life: and I will dwell in the house of the Lord for ever (Ps. 23:5, 6).

And the whole multitude of the people were praying without at the time of incense (Luke 1:10).

And, behold, there talked with Him two men, which were Moses and Elias (Luke 9:30).

GOD'S PROMISE FOR TODAY

Yea, though I walk through the valley of the shadow of death, I will fear no evil: for Thou art with me: Thy rod and Thy staff they comfort me (Ps. 23:4).

"When you corner an opossum he plays dead; when you corner a hypocrite he plays alive."

DECEMBER 23

Fret not thyself because of evildoers, neither be thou envious against the workers of iniquity. For they shall soon be cut down like the grass, and wither as the green herb. Trust in the Lord, and do good; so shalt thou dwell in the land, and verily thou shalt be fed. Delight thyself also in the Lord; and He shall give thee the desires of thine heart (Ps. 37:1-4).

And he that keepeth His commandments dwelleth in Him, and He in him (I John 3:24).

And as he reasoned of righteousness, temperance, and judgment to come, Felix trembled, and answered, Go thy way for this time; when I have a convenient season, I will call for thee (Acts 24:25).

Therefore is the kingdom of heaven likened unto a certain king, which would take account of his servants (Matt. 18:23).

GOD'S PROMISE FOR TODAY

Commit thy way unto the Lord; trust also in Him; and He shall bring it to pass (Ps. 37:5).

"Kindness is the language the dumb can speak and the deaf can understand."

As the hart panteth after the water brooks, so panteth my soul after Thee, O God. My soul thirsteth for God, for the living God: when shall I come and appear before God? My tears have been my meat day and night, while they continually say unto me, where is thy God? When I remember these things, I pour out my soul in me: for I had gone with the multitude, I went with them to the house of God, with the voice of joy and praise, with a multitude that kept holyday (Ps. 42:1-4).

And at the ninth hour Jesus cried with a loud voice, saying, Eloi, Eloi, lama sabachthani? which is, being interpreted, My God, My God, why hast Thou forsaken Me? (Mark 15:34).

GOD'S PROMISE FOR TODAY

Why art thou cast down, O my soul? and why art thou disquieted in me? hope thou in God: for I shall yet praise Him for the help of His countenance (Ps. 42:5).

"Beauty without virtue is a rose without fragrance."

And, behold, thou shalt conceive in thy womb, and bring forth a son, and shalt call His name JESUS. (Luke 1:31).

Wherefore God also hath highly exalted Him, and given Him a name which is above every name: That at the name of Jesus, every knee should bow, of things in heaven and things in earth, and things under the earth; and that every tongue should confess that Jesus Christ is Lord, to the glory of God the Father (Phil. 2:9-11).

His eyes were as a flame of fire, and on His head were many crowns and He had a name written, that no man knew, but He Himself (Rev. 19:12).

And He hath on His vesture and on His thigh a name written, KING OF KINGS, AND LORD OF LORDS (Rev. 19:16).

GOD'S PROMISE FOR TODAY

For unto us a child is born, unto us a son is given: and the government shall be upon His shoulder: and His name shall be called Wonderful, Counsellor, The mighty God, The everlasting Father, The Prince of Peace (Isa. 9:6).

" 'Everybody is doing it!' is the national anthem of hell."

My help cometh from the Lord, which made heaven and earth. He will not suffer thy foot to be moved; He that keepeth thee will not slumber. Behold, he that keepeth Israel shall neither slumber nor sleep. The Lord is thy keeper: the Lord is thy shade upon thy right hand. The sun shall not smite thee by day, nor the moon by night. The Lord shall preserve thee from all evil: He shall preserve thy soul. The Lord shall preserve thy going out and thy coming in from this time forth, and even for evermore (Ps. 121:2-8).

O Ephraim, what shall I do unto thee? O Judah, what shall I do unto thee? for your goodness is as a morning cloud, and as the early dew it goeth away (Hos. 6:4).

Paul, filled with the Holy Ghost, set his eyes on Him (Acts 13:9).

GOD'S PROMISE FOR TODAY

I will lift up mine eyes unto the hills, from whence cometh my help (Ps. 121:1).

"In the straight and narrow path the traffic is all one way."

My son, if thou wilt receive My words, and hide My commandments with thee; so that thou incline thine ear unto wisdom, and apply thine heart to understanding: yea, if thou criest after knowledge, and liftest up thy voice for understanding; if thou seekest her as silver and searchest for her as for hid treasures; then shalt thou understand the fear of the Lord, and find the knowledge of God (Prov. 2:1-5).

And they that use this world, as not abusing it: for the fashion of this world passeth away (I Cor. 7:31).

For whosoever will save his life shall lose it; but whosoever shall lose his life for My sake and the gospel's, the same shall save it (Mark 8:35).

Knowing this, that our old man is crucified with Him, that the body of sin might be destroyed, that henceforth we should not serve sin (Rom. 6:6).

GOD'S PROMISE FOR TODAY

For the Lord giveth wisdom: out of His mouth cometh knowledge of God (Prov. 2:6).

"The more abundant life comes by the death route."

Who hath believed our report? and to whom is the arm of the Lord revealed? For He shall grow up before him as a tender plant, and as a root out of a dry ground: He hath no form nor comeliness; and when we shall see Him, there is no beauty that we should desire Him. He is despised and rejected of men; a man of sorrows, and acquainted with grief: and we hid as it were our faces from Him; He was despised, and we esteemed Him not. Surely He hath borne our griefs, and carried our sorrows: yet we did esteem Him stricken, smitten of God, and afflicted (Isa. 53:1-4).

All we like sheep have gone astray; we have turned every one to his own way; and the Lord hath laid on Him the iniquity of us all (Isa. 53:6).

GOD'S PROMISE FOR TODAY

But He was wounded for our transgressions, He was bruised for our iniquities: the chastisement of our peace was upon Him; and with His stripes we are healed (Isa. 53:5).

"When a boy sows his wild oats it is time for his father to 'thresh.'"

For as the rain cometh down, and the snow from heaven, and returneth not thither, but watereth the earth, and maketh it bring forth and bud, that it may give seed to the sower, and bread to the eater; so shall My word be that goeth forth out of My mouth: it shall not return unto Me void, but it shall accomplish that which I please, and it shall prosper in the thing whereto I sent it. For ye shall go out with joy, and be led forth with peace: the mountains and the hills shall break forth before you into singing, and all the trees of the field shall clap their hands. Instead of the thorn shall come up the fir tree: and it shall be to the Lord for a name, for an everlasting sign that shall not be cut off (Isa. 55:10-13).

GOD'S PROMISE FOR TODAY

For My thoughts are not your thoughts, neither are your ways My ways, saith the Lord. For as the heavens are higher than the earth, so are My ways higher than your ways, and My thoughts than your thoughts (Isa. 55:8, 9).

"Tomorrow is the time when our worries look most ridiculous."

DECEMBER 30

Honour thy father and mother; which is the first commandment with promise (Eph. 6:2).

Servants, be obedient to them that are your masters according to the flesh, with fear and trembling, in singleness of your heart, as unto Christ (Eph. 6:5).

With good will doing service, as to the Lord, and not to men: knowing that whatsoever good thing any man doeth, the same shall he receive of the Lord, whether he be bond or free (Eph. 6:7, 8).

Finally, my brethren, be strong in the Lord, and in the power of His might (Eph. 6:10).

And being in an agony He prayed more earnestly: and His sweat was as it were great drops of blood falling down to the ground (Luke 22:44).

GOD'S PROMISE FOR TODAY

Stand therefore, having your loins girt about with truth, and having on the breastplate of righteousness (Eph. 6:14).

"Home courtesy frequently departs with the guests."

DECEMBER 31

If ye then be risen with Christ, seek those things which are above, where Christ sitteth on the right hand of God. Set your affection on things above, not on things on the earth. For ye are dead, and your life is hid with Christ in God. When Christ, Who is our life, shall appear, then shall ye also appear with Him in glory (Col. 3:1-4).

Let the word of Christ dwell in you richly in all wisdom; teaching and admonishing one another in psalms and hymns and spiritual songs, singing with grace in your hearts to the Lord (Col. 3:16).

For before that certain came from James, he did eat with the Gentiles: but when they were come, he withdrew and separated himself, fearing them which were of the circumcision (Gal 2:12).

GOD'S PROMISE FOR TODAY

And whatsoever ye do in word or deed, do all in the name of the Lord Jesus, giving thanks to God and the Father by Him (Col. 3:17).

"Example is not the main thing in influencing others. It is the only thing."

A MOMENT IN THE MORNING

A moment in the morning,
  Take your Bible in your hand,
And catch a glimpse of glory
  From the peaceful promised land:

It will linger still before you
  When you seek the busy mart,
And like flowers of hope will blossom
  Into beauty in your heart.

The precious words, like jewels,
  Will glisten all the day
With a rare effulgent glory
  That will brighten all the way.

—Arthur Lewis Tubbs

Be strong and of a good courage; be not afraid, neither be thou
dismayed: for the Lord thy God is with thee whithersoever thou
goest (Josh. 1:9).

THE ANVIL OF GOD'S WORD

Last eve I paused beside a blacksmith's door
  And heard the anvil ring the vesper chime;
Then, looking in, I saw upon the floor
  Old hammers worn with beating years of time.

"How many anvils have you had?" said I,
  "To wear and batter all these hammers, so."
"Just one," said he; then said, with twinkling eye,
  "The anvil wears the hammers out, you know."

And so, I thought, the anvil of God's Word
  For ages skeptic blows have beat upon:
Yet, though the noise of falling blows was heard
  The anvil is unharmed—the hammers, gone!

We may boldly say, The Lord is my helper, and I will not fear
what man shall do unto me (Heb. 13:6).

OUR RIGHT TO GOD'S PROMISES

One of Satan's most subtle devices is to dull the Christian sword, or strike it right out of his hand. Satan renders ineffective "the sword of the Spirit, which is the word of God" (Eph. 6:17) by various devices. He either keeps men in ignorance of its existence, or overlays it with such incrustations that its sharp edges are of no use. But with the real saint, who cannot be touched by either of these tricks, he secretly uses another. As Satan goes about seeking whom he may devour, he finds, let us say, a hard-pressed Christian worker lying awake in the small hours of the morning. This man is conscientious, he wants above all things to do the will of God but he keeps turning over in his mind the mistakes and failures of recent days and weeks, and even sins long past and forgiven loom up before him; and one problem after another, which he thinks he will soon have to meet, rises up in the path ahead. The worker knows the Word, so he lays hold of some Old Testament promise, such as this: "Fear thou not; for I am with thee: be not dismayed; for I am thy God: I will strengthen thee; yea, I will help thee; yea, I will uphold thee with the right hand of my righteousness" (Isa. 41:10). Then Satan cuts under the Christian's defense, as it were, and says, "But that promise is not for you—it was spoken by Isaiah to the Jews, and you have no right to it." And unless the Christian warrior has learned how to parry this terrible thrust, he may be sorely wounded. But there is a remedy, so let him hold fast to his sword and use it boldly. Hear these brave words of the warrior Paul, who was not ignorant of Satan's devices: "For whatsoever things were written aforetime were written for our learning, that we through patience and comfort of the Scriptures might have hope" (Rom. 15:4); and, best of all, "For all the promises of God in him are yea, and in him Amen, unto the glory of God by us" (2 Cor. 1:20). Certainly there are promises given to the Jews which relate to material things and are not for us who are the spiritual seed of Abraham. But if God was faithful and merciful to Israel, only because of His love for them, how much more reason have we to rest on the faithfulness of Him who gave His beloved Son for us! "He that spared not his own Son, but delivered him up for us all, how shall he not with him also freely give us all things?" (Rom. 8:32).

Sunday School Times

PRAYER PROMISES

Draw nigh to God and He will draw nigh to you (James 4:8).

If ye abide in Me, and My words abide in you, ye shall ask what ye will, and it shall be done unto you (John 15:7).

What things soever ye desire, when ye pray, believe that ye receive them, and ye shall have them (Mark 11:24).

If two of you shall agree on earth as touching anything that they shall ask, it shall be done for them of my Father which is in heaven (Matt. 18:19).

Have not I commanded thee? be strong and of a good courage (Josh. 1:9).

If we ask anything according to His will, He heareth us (I John 5:14).

And if we know that He heareth us, . . . we know that we have the petitions that we desired (I John 5:15).

Whatsoever we ask, we receive of Him, because we keep His commandments, and do those things that are pleasing in His sight (I John 3:22).

WHAT TO READ

For Comfort

The Lord is good, a strong hold in the day of trouble; and He knoweth them that trust Him (Nah. 1:7).

Call upon Me in the day of trouble: I will deliver thee, and thou shalt glorify Me (Ps. 50:15).

He knoweth the way that I take: when He hath tried me, I shall come forth as gold (Job 23:10).

And we know all things work together for good to them that love God (Rom. 8:28).

He that dwelleth in the secret place of the most high shall abide under the shadow of the Almighty (Ps. 91:1).

When in Need of Encouragement

In all thy ways acknowledge Him, and He shall direct thy paths (Prov. 3:6).

Only be thou strong and very courageous . . . that thou mayest prosper whithersoever thou goest (Josh. 1:7).

Let us therefore come boldly unto the throne of grace, that we may obtain mercy, and find grace to help in time of need (Heb. 4:16).

When Despondent

Cast thy burden upon the Lord, and He shall sustain thee (Ps. 55:22).

He said unto me, my grace is sufficient for thee (II Cor. 12:9).

Casting all your care upon Him; for He careth for you (I Peter 5:7).

I the Lord thy God will hold thy right hand, saying unto thee, Fear not: I will help thee (Isa. 41:13).

THE PLAN OF SALVATION

All Are Sinners

For all have sinned, and come short of the glory of God (Rom. 3:23).

As it is written, there is none righteous, no, not one (Rom. 3:10).

All we like sheep have gone astray; we have turned every one to his own way; and the Lord hath laid on Him the iniquity of us all (Isa. 53:6).

God's Remedy for Sin

For I delivered unto you first of all that which I also received, how that Christ died for our sins according to the Scriptures; and that He was buried, and that He rose again the third day according to the Scriptures (I Cor. 15:3-4).

For He hath made Him to be sin for us, who knew no sin; that we might be made the righteousness of God in Him (II Cor. 5:21).

In whom we have redemption through His blood, the forgiveness of sins, according to the riches of His grace (Eph. 1:7).

All May Be Saved Now

For whosoever shall call upon the name of the Lord shall be saved (Rom. 10:13).

For by grace are ye saved through faith; and that not of yourselves; it is the gift of God: not of works, lest any man should boast (Eph. 2:8-9).

For God so loved the world that He gave His only begotten Son, that whosoever believeth in Him should not perish, but have everlasting life (John 3:16).

MY DECISION FOR CHRIST

Confessing to God that I am a sinner, and believing that the Lord Jesus Christ died for my sins on the cross and was raised for my justification, I do now receive and confess Him as my personal Saviour.

Name_____

Date_____

MY PRAYER LIST